The
English
Couples
— HANDBOOK —

**MIKE AND KATEY
MORRIS**

CROSSWAY BOOKS
CAMBRIDGE

Production and Printing in England for
CROSSWAY BOOKS
Kingfisher House, 7 High Green, Great Shelford,
Cambridge CB2 1SG by
Nuprint Ltd, Station Road, Harpenden, Herts AL5 4SE.

Contents

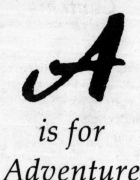

is for
Adventure

THE DAY IS SET. Invitations are chosen, written and sent. Tours of likely hotels and halls for the reception are completed and the final choice has been made. Final adjustments are made to her dress and a desperate search is carried out for a suit that fits him. Wedding rings need to be chosen. There's always something we forget.

Sounds familiar? It's the well-worn path countless couples have travelled as they prepare to enter 'the estate of holy matrimony' or marriage as it is more commonly described.

What lies the other side of the 'big day' as everyone insists on calling it, with a knowing look in their eye and a strange leer of the lip? Certainly the preparations are fun, but they are also exhausting and sometimes extremely stressful. Indeed, the very energy required in setting up the day can obscure our focus on the marriage which is to follow. Several months of expectation, concentration and hard work building towards an occasion will give way to a lifetime together.

Have we got what it takes? Do we have any idea what it will require? Has our experience in our parental home

4

been happy? Is there a role model for us to follow or are we learning from scratch?

Many couples today do not have a very positive picture of marriage to carry with them as they begin a committed relationship, and in many cases one blessed by the church in a service which has more to do with tradition than a meaningful kick-off to the marriage. And yet the truth is each partner's mind is filled with questions. Will it last? If it doesn't work out, can I get a divorce? Am I becoming a piece of property—losing my independence and individuality?

That's the great thing about marriage. It is an adventure; and what adventurer ever knows on setting out if they will complete the challenge before them? So with marriage; it is a challenge. A journey that will require great stamina and strength from both partners. An adventure which has the capacity to become the most exciting and challenging task ever undertaken by two individuals, one which will demand sacrifice, develop character and enrich each person's experience of life. The challenge of the adventure called marriage is whether together the couple can discover the resources to complete the course successfully.

Each couple will face different set backs. No two marriages are the same. Circumstances will vary and yet the objective is the same: to stay together, discovering that neither could have chosen a route leading to a more fulfilled experience of life.

In the next few pages we hope to provide helpful insights for those preparing to take the plunge. These emerge from our own experience and from talking to countless couples both before they marry and following them through the heights and depths of their marriage experience.

Organised as an 'A—Z', it is aimed to become a helpful bedside reference book for the months leading up to the wedding and also, we dare to suggest, into the first few years of marital bliss. The advice given is very practical; from bride's hairdo to contraceptive wisdom. It is our hope that the few words of encouragement found in this book will prove helpful as you struggle to resolve that first argument; weep as the tension builds towards the wedding day; sort out with whose parents Christmas will be spent.

Each section is short, punchy and easily read. Where appropriate, basic guidelines are provided, for example in how to find a mortgage or budgeting the household finance week by week.

Albert Einstein, the famous scientist, once expressed the view that the average person only ever uses 10% of his mental powers. We believe that many couples only ever achieve the same percentage of their marriage potential. Just as improving the mind takes a measure of disciplined commitment, so does marriage. No relationship just happens.

Marriage should be seen as an ongoing, lifetime relationship. Each partner is an equal shareholder, equally responsible for the shape and direction of the relationship and equally committed, no matter what the circumstances or discoveries along the way. When we discovered that we had a less than 1% chance of having children, our commitment to each other and hence our marriage was tested. Our marriage withstood, and is withstanding, the test but only due to a level of commitment attained through honest talking and learning to understand and appreciate each other in new ways.

When pressure comes, as indeed it will, it is important to remember that you need your partner at that point. There is no room for a mindset that sees a failure and a need to start again. No; rather as obstacles are encountered during the voyage of discovery marriage provides, the partners together find the way to overcome and go on. It is more a continuous journey than a series of episodes. Just as a car will tend to fail you at the most inopportune time unless it is regularly serviced, so a marriage will run into problems unless it receives constant maintenance; and both wife and husband are the mechanics. Though there may be times when the help of the marriage garage may be appropriate!

As you read and consider the following pages please remember we do not have a series of solutions; rather, helpful principles which we have discovered and practise ourselves. They have also been taken up and used by many other couples we have had the privilege of preparing for marriage.

As you move into marriage remember the experience of Christopher Columbus who set out not knowing where he was going, arrived not knowing where he was and returned not knowing where he'd been. In this way he discovered America. I bet he'd have appreciated an 'A—Z' guide to recognising foreign countries. This is the Christopher Columbus guide to marriage. Do yourself a favour and start reading.

Before reading further, however, complete the following questions and discuss your answers with your partner.

A. Why do you think now is the right time to marry? (Tick as many as you like.)

☐1. I'm old enough
☐2. I'm in love
☐3. I want to leave home
☐4. I've found the right person
☐5. I can afford it
☐6. Most of my friends are engaged or married
☐7. I want security
☐8. The sooner I'm married the better
☐9. I could never find anyone else as nice

B. Of all the boyfriends/girlfriends I've known my partner is special because ....
C. In what ways do you think you will be happier as a married person than as a single person?

is for Bride

THE WEDDING DAY is often said to be 'the Bride's Day'. The bride is certainly the centre of attention in many ways. It is also a very special day for the bride's parents, not least because they are seeing their daughter leave their care to start a new life with someone else. This is true even if the bride to be has been living away from her childhood home for several years. The bride's mother has usually been very involved with all the preparations for the wedding day, so in many ways it can be seen as her day too.

There are many factors to occupy the bride's mind and energy in the run up to the wedding, and many things must be considered in plenty of time.

The dress

The wedding dress is usually the most expensive single item necessary for the day, but do not panic; you need not buy. There are a few options available:

(a) Buy a gown
(b) Hire a gown

    (c) Make a gown
    (d) Borrow a gown

A dress which is bought will obviously belong to the bride. However, ask yourself what you will do with the dress after the wedding day. It may be altered so that it can be used again (perhaps as a baby gown), kept for posterity or sold.

There are many specialist shops where you can buy your dress—national chains and local independent stores. Department stores often have a bridal department too. Trying on wedding dresses can be great fun but it is also tiring. Make sure you are wearing white underwear, and take someone with you who will be level headed and honest about the dresses you try on. It helps to have a second opinion apart from the assistant who is probably trying to sell you the most expensive dress in the range!

A dress which is hired works out more economical for one day's wear. And you may be able to choose a style which is more extravagant. There is no problem about what to do with it after the big event. *Yellow Pages* lists hire companies, national and local, under Wedding Services.

A dress which is made can be made to fit exactly (as long as the bride's weight doesn't fluctuate dramatically near the wedding day!). It can include personal touches (like royal wedding dresses often do) and can also be tailored to suit the purse.

Borrowing a gown is also a viable option, similar to hiring. There may be a particular gown which is, or is becoming, a family heirloom. A friend may have a gown which you particularly admire and would enjoy wearing on your wedding day. This is often the cheapest approach to acquiring a wedding dress but provision must be made for cleaning the gown afterwards.

However you acquire your dress it is important to try it on with the other accessories, ie underwear and shoes. The height of the shoes should take into consideration your height, the groom's height and also comfort. It's a long day with a lot of standing, so it is important to be comfortable. It may be romantic to wear a garter but be sure it doesn't show through your dress, particularly if the garter is black!

It's not essential to wear a traditional wedding gown. They can be expensive and of very limited use so you may decide to wear a smart dress or suit which will be serviceable afterwards. Remember, it's your day so you can wear what you want to.

Hair

Hair is a very important component of our overall appearance. Obviously the headdress will dictate what hairstyle will be worn on the wedding day. Again there are various options:

(a) A veil which can be worn over the face at the beginning of the service and then off the face
(b) A veil which is off the face all the time
(c) A hat
(d) A headdress without a veil
(e) No headwear

Once the decision about headgear is made, plans should be made concerning hair dressing. If you are planning a radical change for the wedding day a rehearsal is essential. Perhaps you are planning to have a perm. If so, one to two months before the wedding would be a good idea. If you are having a trial run, we would encourage you to take your headgear to show the hairdresser so that he/she knows what the final aim is. Katey had fresh flowers in her hair and she practised with the comb to which they were attached. Remember that life does continue after the wedding service so plan how you will wear your hair when going away. Katey's hair had been so severely lacquered that she had no option!

Make-up

If you are wearing a traditional gown which is full length and white you need to adjust your make-up accordingly. One full rehearsal is essential so that you know what you are doing. Many hair salons also offer a make-up service, as do many department stores. The choice is yours but it is important to book hair and/or beauty treatments well in advance. Don't forget that bridesmaids will also need to be beautified!

Some hairdressers and make-up specialists will come to the house. This can save a lot of hassle and unnecessary travelling on a busy day.

Bride's timetable

The details of every wedding day are different but there are some 'landmarks' which are always there. This timetable is for a 1.30pm wedding but adjustments can easily be made to fit in with your day.

8.00am	Get up. Breakfast and bath. Time with family.
9.30am	Pick up headdress of fresh flowers and fresh flowers for top of the wedding cake from the florist. Deliver cake flowers to the reception venue.
10.00am	Arrive for hair and make-up appointment. Hair washed, make-up applied, hair styled and headdress fitted.
11.00am	Driven from hairdressers to home where a light lunch is consumed.
12.00pm	Bridesmaids arrive to get ready. Bride and bridesmaids help each other with bride's mother.
12.45pm	Bride gets into dress. Leave this as late as possible to avoid accidents.
1.00pm	Various photographss taken at bride's home, eg bride, bridesmaids and bride's parents.

11

1.10pm	Bridesmaids and bride's mother leave for the church.
1.20pm	Car returns to pick up bride and father.
1.30pm	Bride and father arrive at church.

Behaviour

In celluloid epics the bride is often portrayed as a 'spoiled brat' ruling the roost on 'her' day, getting all and sundry that she requests, whether reasonable or not.

A bride should remember that the wedding day can be traumatic for her parents. They have cared for the bride since babyhood and now they are witnessing her about to begin a new life in a home of her own with another man. Parents therefore need to be treated gently with sensitivity, even though the bride also needs careful treatment. It is a good idea to celebrate together in the morning over events like breakfast. Perhaps with a little thought the bride can make this an extraordinary time with special touches.

A mother often likes to perform a last duty to her daughter by helping her dress and prepare. The father also enjoys the special time when he and his daughter travel alone to the wedding. These are often treasured memories the bride will take with her into marriage.

It is a lovely touch for the bride and groom to acknowledge what they owe to their parents by presenting each set of parents with a small gift. This can be done at the reception, at a private meal just before the great day or at some other time when parents and children are together.

A bride should aim at making this a day to remember for everyone involved. This can be done with just a little forethought.

Flowers

Traditionally brides carry a bouquet of flowers. The time of year and the amount of money you wish to spend will govern what flowers you choose. Florists usually have photos of bouquets they have made up and will also advise on choice of flowers. The shape of the bouquets for bride and bridesmaids needs to be considered as well. A small bridesmaid often copes better with a ball of flowers on a ribbon rather than a bouquet. Baskets or hoops are other popular alternatives. These days silk flowers which are, of course, everlasting are very popular—especially if the bride wants to keep her bouquet.

Buttonholes for the men involved should also be ordered well in advance. The colour and the type of flower need to be decided upon. A colour contrasting with or matching, for example, the bridesmaids dresses can help to give a co-ordinating look. Buttonholes or corsages should be provided for each set of parents, best man and ushers. More can be provided. The list is open-ended but grandparents and godparents are often included, as are special friends or anyone who has been particularly involved in the wedding.

Do turn to 'W is for Wedding Day' for a full explanation of all participants' responsibilities running up to and on the day of the wedding itself.

C

is for Contraception

A REGULAR SEX LIFE is an essential ingredient to a satisfying and healthy marriage. If there are problems in this area please turn to 'S is for Sex'.

Our forefathers (or should it be foremothers?) demonstrated this by the fact that it was quite normal for a child to be born every year. Today, we are not so much in the lap of the gods. We have the benefits of contraception. But it is not always plain sailing.

Contraception, the means by which we seek to prevent the fertilisation of the female's egg by the male's sperm, should be openly and fully discussed by every engaged couple. This must be done in good time before the wedding so that plans can be acted upon before the honeymoon. It is not now so socially acceptable to bear a child every nine months; nor can many couples afford it.

Discussing contraception and the sexual dynamic of your relationship will provoke a healthy discussion about children. Do you like and want children of your own? In an ideal world, when would this be? Are there financial implications for your lifestyle and aspirations? What are they? It would be appropriate to turn to 'O is for Offspring' at this point for further discussion on the subject of children.

Contraception can appear a very confusing subject at first glance. However, be assured there is a lot of useful advice available to you both. We stress *both* since you will both be involved in sex, so it is as much his as her responsibility. Somehow, because most contraceptives apart from the sheath involve women, men seem to think it is a matter for women only. This is untrue. Men should accompany their wife to be to the GP or family planning clinic to be as involved as possible in this part of preparing for marriage.

Books

These provide a useful source of information. There are many free pieces of literature available from your GP or family planning clinic and you would be well advised to get hold of these. Some books cover specific forms of contraception. Reading widely can present you with conflicting information, for example on the side-effects of the pill, so make sure you can take your questions to your doctor or that you can handle the various viewpoints. Your local library will have a number of books that you can borrow or any good bookshop should carry some.

Friends

Close friends in whom we have confidence are also a great asset. They can hopefully speak from experience and give personal insights. This is often more reassuring than any piece of literature or the GP with whom we may not be especially relaxed.

GP/family planning clinic

This is one visit you should certainly make; if only for the free samples! Here you can talk through all the various

15

methods of contraception, what is involved, their reliability in preventing conception and any possible side-effects. They will be able to instruct you in their use and their suitability for you.

Some of the more 'mechanical' methods such as the IUD will need to be professionally fitted, which will be done on just such a visit.

A woman asking for family planning advice will almost certainly be given a full internal examination. This is nothing to be anxious about and it does help to relax for it. This is purely a routine measure. Indeed, in the years ahead an internal will become the norm for checking that cervical cancer has not found its way into your system.

Methods available

So what are the methods of contraception available to us? Consider the following chart to get an outline of methods, suitability, practical use and reliability.

Methods of birth control

Method	Who for?	Medical advice needed?	Reliable?	Comments
The Pill	Her	Yes	Very	Not suitable for all women
Intrauterine Device (IUD) (permanently fitted in womb)	Her	Yes	Very	Fitted by doctor– only yearly check needed. Removed by doctor when you want a baby
Cap	Her	Yes	Very– especially when used with spermicidal cream	Doctor or nurse chooses right size. Put in vagina before intercourse.

Sterilization	Him/her	Yes	Completely–permanent	Operation required. Only suitable when family complete
Condom (sheath)	Him	No	Fairly	Can be purchased at most chemists or prescribed by Family Planning doctor
Creams, foams, jellies	Her	No	Moderately	Available at chemists and Family Planning centres
Safe period		No	Only if calculated on a regular cycle	Advice and special temperature charts etc. from FPA or CMAC

You can find the address of your local Family Planning Clinic in the telephone directory. Drop in or phone during the hours that your clinic is open and make an appointment.

The pill. There are different types of pill available. The pill must be prescribed by a doctor. Taking the pill regularly means that you should have your blood pressure tested from time to time.

The pill is taken by the woman every day for twenty-one days. During the following seven days the woman will menstruate. On the twenty-ninth day (day one of the next cycle) a new packet of pills is started.

The pill works by suppressing ovulation and is a highly reliable method of contraception providing the woman remembers to take it. It is also the husband's responsibility to remind her.

There may be a few side-effects since the pill does not suit everyone. However, your GP can advise you here and even let you try out different types of pill to find one that suits you.

Aesthetically the pill is the most pleasing form of contraceptive. However, some women can't get on with it or carry anxieties about health risks that have been identified with it in the press. Therefore you must decide if you are both happy with this method before proceeding. If you do adopt the pill as your method of contraception then it is a good idea to begin taking it three months before your wedding day so that any problems can be dealt with and you are comfortable with it as you depart for your honeymoon.

Intra-Uterine Device (IUD or coil). An IUD is a mechanical device inserted into the woman. It must be fitted by a doctor and stays in place permanently. It should be checked annually. Some people have a moral problem with IUDs because they enable conception to take place before preventing the egg embedding in the lining of the uterus. Again, an IUD is painless and makes no difference to sexual intercourse. It is also very reliable.

The cap. The cap is another method of contraception to be used by the wife. It is carefully fitted so that it fits tightly into the vagina thus preventing any of the man's semen entering into the woman and leading to fertilisation. It must be inserted into the vagina prior to intercourse. This can be done as a matter of course every night or can be incorporated into lovemaking. It should be used with spermicidal cream to make it more effective and should be left in position for some hours after intercourse. This can be a very effective method of contraception.

Sterilisation. The husband or the wife can be sterilised. It is a smaller, more straightforward operation for the man involving local anaesthetic, whereas for a woman it is quite a major operation. This method of contraception is 100% effective and should be considered to be irreversible. It is not a method of contraception which should be considered by young newly weds.

Sheath. The sheath or condom is a method of contraception used by the man. Sheaths are widely available at chemists and most supermarkets. They are also available at family planning clinics. The sheath is fitted over the man's erect penis. The idea is for it to contain the man's semen thus preventing conception. Condoms should be used in conjunction with spermicides to ensure a higher level of contraceptive protection. Some people find condoms a real 'turn off' because they appear to be so very unnatural but others find them very acceptable.

Creams, foams and jellies. These are available at chemists and family planning centres and need no medical advice. They are used by the woman but some find them messy and therefore distasteful. They are only moderately reliable.

Safe period. The safe period relies on accurate prediction of when the woman ovulates. By avoiding intercourse around that time conception is avoided. It is very helpful if the woman has a regular monthly cycle! No medical advice is needed but advice and a special temperature chart are available from the Catholic Marriage Advisory Council (see *Yellow Pages* for address and phone number). The woman must take her temperature every morning before she gets up and plot it on a graph. Upon ovulation the temperature rises and stays at the higher level. A benefit of this method is that it is completely natural. If used carefully, and calculations are made accurately, it can be a good and fairly reliable method of contraception.

Whichever method of contraception you decide to use, it is important that you both assume corporate responsibility for the situation. Each method puts more responsibility on one of the partners but it is still a joint responsibility.

Some couples do decide to give contraception a miss and leave it up to God. If you decide to do this, you must be prepared to have a child nine months after you marry!

D

is for
Daily Budgeting

IN 'F IS FOR FINANCE' we will take a full look at the whole area of money matters. However, this section deals with the issue of money management. Every day we need to spend cash. Housekeeping, necessities, luxuries: all demand our income. There is nothing wrong with this but if we do not monitor it carefully it will run away with us.

Money cannot look after itself. It is an essential friend and a ruthless enemy. Once our financial affairs begin to get out of hand we are often fighting a losing battle to recover solvency and order in our financial affairs.

Money management is a vital skill that we all need to acquire. If, like Mike, you are innumerate, never fear. There are very practical guidelines to be followed and they are explained in this section. Furthermore, it only takes one of you to manage the money side of the relationship. Nevertheless, both of you must be able to take over from each other at a moment's notice.

For either partner not to know your joint financial situation is unacceptable within marriage. All income is joint no matter who earns it; no matter who generates the most. For years Katey earned more than Mike but he was happy to be a kept man. In real terms though we both knew what our financial position was, where the loot was stashed, and each had access to all accounts.

If you have not done so before, answer the following questions together with your partner.

A. My wage/salary each week/month is ....
B. My savings amount to £................................
C. My bank is ....
D. My account is a
  (1) Current account
  (2) Deposit account
  (3) Other (please specify)
E. My other accounts, eg building society, are ....
  (please specify).
F. My shares are .... (list all shares together with values and average dividend payments).

It is as well to start as you mean to continue and there should be no financial secrets between you. If you have financial liabilities as a result of family, friends or business connections you should also come clean on those so that your partner knows precisely what (s)he is marrying into. Lack of clarity at this stage on this issue can lead to difficulties not long into marriage itself.

One of the key things about money is that it needs constant attention. While this may be obvious if you are trading with billions on the stock market, it is equally true that your rather small household budget requires regular attention. However, we are often very sloppy in this whole area of money management.

We are all aware of what happens if we neglect the family car. One day we leave the house, climb into the vehicle, turn the ignition key and nothing happens. If a car is not regularly serviced, don't be surprised if it fails you; and usually at the most inconvenient moment.

So it is with our family finances. Ignore them, or assume the bank manager is keeping a helpful eye over your financial affairs, and you will end up in trouble.

What's required is some practical administration of your financial affairs.

Income

First, you will need to establish the total income you and your partner are receiving. Then you will have to calculate your expenditure before comparing the two and discovering if you can afford to live!

To compute your earnings, both you and your fiancée should consult your pay slips which you should receive from your employer. This gives you a lot of information but all you are interested in is the net or take home figure. This relates to the amount of cash put into your hand at the end of each week or deposited in your bank account at month's end.

If you are paid monthly multiply the net figure by twelve to see how much you earn in a year. This is purely for your own information as we will be working on the monthly sums for the purposes of this section. On the other hand, if you are paid weekly then multiply your weekly income by fifty two (number of weeks in a year and hence your annual take home pay) before dividing by twelve (the number of months in a year thereby giving you an average monthly income figure).

$£** \times 52 = ? \div 12 = ?$ average monthly income

There may be other sources of income which are received on a regular basis (social security benefits, child allowance, building society interest, shares, etc). All these figures need to be entered in; but remember: average them out over the year so that you get a monthly average. The following chart will help you here.

Item	Amount earned	Payment date	Average monthly value
Employment:			
Husband			
Wife			
U/e benefit			
Other benefits:			
(a)			
(b)			
(c)			
(d)			
Building society interest			
Share div.			
Other			
TOTAL			

Obviously, if you are self-employed your earnings may be more difficult to establish but from your previous books you should be in a position to set down your average monthly income.

Expenditure

When it comes to the money you spend each month (your outgoings) there are two aspects to consider: regular and irregular payments. Now by 'irregular' we do not mean backhanders, so do not be alarmed!

Regular expenditure is the payment of set amounts which are made each month such as your mortgage repayments. The only variant here is the rate of interest charged and you will be forewarned about any increase in payments.

Irregular expenditure includes fuel bills (higher in winter than in summer), house repairs, Christmas, etc. You might also include trips to the dentist and the like here which may prove an unexpected extra one month. This irregularity of outgoings explains why one month you are apparently wealthy, enjoying a surplus, and the next you are in deficit!

Practical and simple administration of your finances can iron out hiccups and enable you to be aware of an anticipated surplus and therefore utilise it to cover the known deficit in another month.

Having listed your income, you should now work through the following charts and assess as accurately as possible your expenditure. Before you do so, however, you will need to approximate some of your irregular outgoings. You may not spend what you allocate but at least you won't be spending money you haven't allowed for.

To make this approximation look at last year's bills, or if you are buying or renting a property request the vendor or landlord to give you the figures and adding them together divide by twelve to give you a monthly average. Do likewise for other anticipated expenditure. Decide on a sum to cover the cost of birthday presents for example, then divide by twelve and see what the average monthly total is. Obviously you won't spend that amount each month but you will be able to compare your average monthly expenditure with your average monthly income.

Now complete the following tables.

AVERAGE MONTHLY EXPENDITURE

ITEM	Amount paid	How often	Date of payment	Who is paid	Amount/ mth	Notes
Rent/Mortgage	£				£	
Rates	£				£	
Water rates	£				£	
Ground rent	£				£	
Service charge	£				£	

Community charge	£	£
Insurance schemes	£	£
Pension fund	£	£
Electricity	£	£
Gas	£	£
Oil	£	£
Coal	£	£
Telephone	£	£
Maintenance payments	£	£
House repairs	£	£
Redecoration	£	£
Car loan	£	£
Car fuel	£	£
MOT	£	£
Road tax	£	£
Vehicle insurance	£	£
Car repairs	£	£
Public transport	£	£
Groceries	£	£
Other housekeeping	£	£
Kid's pocket money	£	£
Childminding	£	£
Pet food	£	£
Vet bills	£	£
Clothing	£	£
Laundry	£	£
Regular prescriptions	£	£
Dentist	£	£
Optician	£	£

TV licence	£	£
TV rental	£	£
Video rental	£	£
Christmas	£	£
Birthday presents	£	£
Holiday	£	£
Trips and outings	£	£
Sporting activities	£	£
Hobbies	£	£
Records and tapes	£	£
Toys and books	£	£
Drinks	£	£
Cigarettes/tobacco	£	£
Newspapers	£	£
Other	£	£
	£	£
	£	£
	£	£
TOTAL	£	£

MONTHLY CREDIT REPAYMENTS

ITEM		Amount paid	How often	Date of payment	Who is paid	Amount/ mth	Notes
Mortgage		£				£	
Second mortgage		£				£	
Secured loans	1	£				£	
	2	£				£	
Unsecured loans	1	£				£	
	2	£				£	
	3	£				£	

Credit cards	1	£	£	
	2	£	£	
	3	£	£	
	4	£	£	
Storecards	1	£	£	
	2	£	£	
	3	£	£	
	4	£	£	
Catalogues	1	£	£	
	2	£	£	
	3	£	£	
Local moneylender		£	£	
Hire purchase	1	£	£	
	2	£	£	
Others		£	£	
		£	£	
		£	£	
		£	£	
		£	£	
TOTAL		£	£	

You are now in a position to do some simple sums. Take your combined totals from your expenditure table and debt repayment table, add them together and subtract their combined total from your income total. If you still have money to spare then you are in credit and are living within your means. If not then you need to do a bit of pruning.

Pruning

What we mean here is that if you are spending more than you are earning when you have completed the above steps, then you need to return to your expenditure table

27

to prune it. Work through each item and identify what is essential expenditure and what is unessential. It is the unessential items that will need to be cut. For example, fuel is an essential item but clothing can be trimmed. We have also found that when under financial pressure, working hard at when we have hot water and the amount of heating we have on during the day makes a significant difference to the size of the fuel bills.

Work through your expenditure table doing some ruthless pruning. Be fair to each other. What you may see as inessential may be life's blood to your partner; therefore work on this together and negotiate. Remember, however, that you are seeking to get to a balanced budget where income meets expenditure.

If you find that you are seriously in debt then seek advice. Your local Citizens' Advice Bureau (details in your phone book, *Yellow Pages* or from your local library) will assist you. Below is a further chart that you should fill in if you find yourself already owing a lot of money that you have previously taken out on credit terms. Complete this if appropriate and take it with you when you visit the CAB.

DEFAULT DEBTS

ITEM	Amount owed	Interest rate (APR)	Notes
Mortgage arrears	£	%	
Second mortgage arrears	£	%	
Secured loan arrears	£	%	
Rent arrears	£	%	
Rates arrears	£	%	
Electricity arrears	£	%	
Gas arrears	£	%	
Outstanding Community Charge	£	%	
Water rates arrears	£	%	

Income tax arrears	£	%
Credit card arrears	£	%
Storecard arrears	£	%
Hire purchase arrears	£	%
VAT arrears	£	%
Unpaid fines	£	%
Maintenance arrears	£	%
Bank overdraft	£	%
Other	£	%
	£	%
	£	%
TOTAL	£	%

When dealing with debt remember to be honest about your situation; first with yourself. It's easy to stick bills unopened into the desk drawer; to continue to live as if you have no financial worries. Admitting to yourself that you have problems is the start to getting rid of them.

Secondly, talk with your partner. They share the consequences and indebtedness anyway. Hopefully you are both fully aware of the household financial state so will be in touch with the debt problem.

Thirdly, let the people to whom you owe money know your situation. Inform your bank manager and also the building society or whomever you have a mortgage with, if you have one at all. It is worth noting that you need to deal with those creditors (the people to whom you owe money) who can take most from you first. The building society could take your house from you. Therefore communicate with them and keep them informed. The CAB will help you devise a plan to organise your debts and seek to protect you and your family as much as is possible.

Controlling your finance

You will need to decide whether you will share a joint account or both operate independent accounts. For years we operated separate accounts because we couldn't effectively regulate a joint one. We found it impossible to co-ordinate our expenditure and we would go overdrawn, with one spending without the other knowing that the balance was reduced. With separate accounts we could take responsibility for avoiding being overdrawn.

We now have a joint account into which both salaries are paid and from which all standing orders are paid. We also have a second joint account to cover housekeeping. Each month a sum is paid over into this account and we can effectively budget the housekeeping. If we only have £10 for the last week of the month, that is all that is spent.

We also operate a joint, high interest building society account with immediate withdrawal facilities which provides us with a means of saving. Rather than buy on credit we save for the purchases we want to make. Katey also has her own building society account into which she pays birthday money and other financial gifts and then spends on what she wants whenever.

All our social spending comes out of the main joint account. In our early years of marriage, Katey operated this and did all the finances. However, she sneakily passed it over to Mike a few years ago and has so far successfully resisted taking it back!

Finally, we do have a high interest, withdrawal with ninety days' notice without penalty, building society account. This is for unexpected sums or when we have a surplus one month. It is for unexpected expenditure, eg a new roof. Every so often we intend to pay off some of our mortgage if it builds up to suitable proportions.

Money saving hints

1. Don't buy cheap clothes! Sounds crazy but Katey's mum always says: 'Poor people can't afford cheap clothes.' Now you may get a bargain but there again it may fall apart within a year. Mike buys quality Clarks shoes with commando soles. He has two pairs; one brown and one black. The brown pair he bought eight years ago and they are still not worn out and have not needed re heeling or soleing. This is good value for money.

2. Don't neglect the second-hand market. Good bargains can be had, but only buy what is useful. A bargain is only such if it is something you need and will use.

3. Buy to suit your income. Is the house you are considering easy to keep warm, easy to maintain and within walking distance of shops and school? Think before you purchase anything. Is it the best and most practical buy?

4. Save now and buy later. Avoid the pitfalls of credit by organising your own regular saving plan and delaying purchase until you have the cash available. Then negotiate a cash discount!

In these ways you can gain control of your money and budget effectively. You may not have the lifestyle that you observe in all the glossy magazines but you will have one that you can afford. As for quality of life, this is always improved through avoidance of debt and all the stress and hassle that it can produce.

We are grateful to the book *Credit & Debt. Sorting it out* by Michael Schluter and David Lee for the tables printed above and would commend this helpful book to you.

is for
Engagement

TRADITIONALLY THIS IS that period of time between asking your girlfriend to marry you and the wedding day itself. Once engaged your partner is known as your fiancé(e).

The actual word 'engaged' refers to a formal promise or covenant. Basically, a commitment has been entered into by the man to marry and take responsibility for the woman. In medival times this period was a most important time. The promise having been accepted it was then the responsibility of the man to demonstrate to his intended's father that he had a job generating sufficient income to provide for his bride following the wedding. She was not at risk from being purloined by someone else since a public commitment had been made.

Today this is no longer the case. It is more a social convention and often the length of the engagement is dictated by the financial needs of the couple in providing accommodation in which to begin their married life. However, it is a special period and there is certainly a change in the intensity and nature of their relationship once people get engaged.

Approaching the intended's father

Although engagement is a far more informal affair today it is quite appropriate to approach the bride's father and request the hand of his daughter in marriage, as the time honoured form of words runs. This is no more than a matter of courtesy and makes a statement about the measure of respect you have for your intended father-in-law. It may therefore have diplomatic aspects to recommend it!

All eager young men should reflect on the fact that many fathers struggle at the thought that they are going to be replaced as the major male decision maker in their daughter's life. The way the proposal is handled can have a marked impact upon the character and quality of the future relationship with the young lady's parents.

Today, with many children growing up in broken families, it may prove more difficult to follow the above course of action. However, be inventive and if your fiancé(e) has been brought up by her mother and there is no real bonding with her natural father then request her mother's permission. The whole object behind the tradition in today's society should be to express respect to the parent(s) and value in the intended.

When we decided to get engaged we chose Christmas Eve. Mike, aware that Katey was particularly concerned about various informal anniversaries, chose carefully, knowing he could remember Christmas Eve. He had learned from frequent failure to recall the date we started going out together when questioned by Katey. The same mistake would not be made again.

A few days before this he visited Katey's father to request his permission to marry her. Knowing Katey was out he arrived on his motorbike, rang the door bell and waited. Katey's father came to the door and immediately informed Mike that his daughter was out. Now Katey's father is somewhat deaf due to an industrial accident. On explaining that he knew Katey was not in her father then asked if there was something wrong with the motorbike. This was a natural question since Mike's knowledge of things mechanical was negligible and Katey's father was an engineer who had proved most helpful in the past. On realising there was no easy entrance to be gained to the house Mike raised his voice and shouted: 'I would like to marry Katey if you are agreeable.'

The whole neighbourhood was informed along with Katey's dad who happily at that point responded: 'I think you had better come in.'

Mike went in, and fortunately Katey's father was in full agreement.

Making the announcement

Once the bride to be's father has been approached, a decision needs to be made about whether an announcement should be placed in the newspapers. This decision is often taken out of the hands of the engaged couple by overjoyed parents who assume all their friends avidly scan the 'hatches, matches and despatches' columns and feel the world in general ought to enjoy their good news.

If you are placing the announcement in the newspaper phone in and get a costing before dictating your chosen form of words. Have this written down before you phone as the paper will take it down during the call, read it back to you, confirm the appearance date and either send you an invoice or take details of a suitable credit card for payment.

Choosing the ring

It is today unusual for the man to arrive with a ring already purchased to place on his betrothed's finger. Strange though it may seem she has quite set ideas about the type of ring, the setting and the stone(s), and enjoys being involved in trying on various rings and making the choice with her intended.

It is worth noting that the lower the carat of the gold the tougher it is and the better it will withstand rubbing against the wedding ring once married.

There are also lovely rings available second hand which will certainly provide financial savings. Alternatively, this is the way to obtain an antique ring if that is your preference.

Increasingly common today is the giving of an engagement present by the girl to her betrothed. This should reflect the financial realities of her situation. A wallet, tie clip or a signet ring are popular choices. This is not however mandatory.

The engagement party

This is traditionally held on the day the engagement is announced. There can be difficulties—especially if the couple hail from different geographical locations. At least seek to get the parents together to celebrate the occasion.

Often the bride's parents meet the costs of this party, though again couples are increasingly taking this responsibility themselves. Traditionally the bride's father makes the announcement of the engagement at a suitable moment. The couple and their friends may well move on to a night club later leaving the family members to continue at a pace more suitable to their age.

Engagement presents

It may well be that family and close friends wish to give you a present to mark the occasion of your engagement. They will often ask if there is anything in particular you would like. Assuming that the wedding is not too far distant it may be appropriate to request one or two small items for your future home together. When we got engaged we received a hand mixer, casserole dishes, brandy glasses and similar items.

However, if finance is the most pressing need don't be afraid to request cheques towards a home of your own or some large item, such as a washing machine.

Being engaged

Once engaged the relationship takes on a whole new feel. There is an increased intensity. Why this should be we do not know but in the majority of cases this is what people testify to. As a result it is important to think through how you intend to handle life during the engagement. This is the final stage of growing towards marriage and habits learned now will be hard to shed later.

There are three fundamental areas you will need to address regarding your relationship. These are the social, the sexual and the spiritual.

Social. By this we mean the maintenance and development of your relationships with your wider circle of friends. It is most unrealistic to believe that your fiancé(e) and future spouse will meet all your social needs. You should seek to retain a good and active contact with your special friends.

Traditionally this has been the preserve of the 'lads': off playing football all winter and cricket all summer, this is frequently interrupted by trips to the pub. However, women also need their free time with their mates and the men must learn to accept and help this to happen.

Then there are those shared friendships. Eating, drinking and generally socialising together creates an important further forum for enriching your relationship. It's amazing how much you learn by observing others. Things you want to emulate, things you want to avoid and things that cause you a sigh of relief because you are not the only ones struggling with a particular issue.

We all need friends. Our partner should be our foremost and best friend. But we do need other friends of the same sex as ourselves with whom we can sound off, seek advice and generally unwind. It is important that we retain a measure of discretion and trustworthiness in such relationships as we are acting as friends and not enemies. Talking over personal conversations with others later is not the action of a friend.

Sit down and talk through how you will work out this social dimension during your engagement. This is a good preparation for marriage and helps you to discover each others views on each other's friendships and the shared social element you want to develop. It also means you don't hive off on your own all the time, increasing the intensity and ultimately the isolation of your relationship.

It may help to list your current friends below and identify those you want to build with together. Then answer the following few questions and discuss your answers.

Her friends   *His friends*   *Our friends*

1. How often do you like to go out socially during the week?
2. Where do you like to go?
3. What does the weekend mean to you?
4. Do you like entertaining at your own place?
5. How much do you spend socially over a week? (Include the cost of entertaining friends at home.)
6. Do you find mixing with new people difficult?
7. Do you like your fiancé(e)'s friends?

8. Is there one friend who acts as a confidante for you?

Once you have thought through your answers, discuss them with your partner, but do avoid a slanging match! Simply learn more about each other. If there are friends of yours whom your partner doesn't like, then seek to establish the reasons why. It may well be that they feel insecure or even threatened by them. Better to learn honestly now than through painful experience later.

Sexual relationship. By this we obviously mean the physical side of the relationship. This is dealt with in far more detail under 'S is for Sex' and 'C is for Contraception' but at this point we want to talk briefly about establishing the parameters for this important side of the relationship.

Although in our society it is now assumed that all couples have sex before they are married, this is not everyone's chosen course. In an age when pornography is so readily available and we appear to have achieved the ultimate in sexual freedom, the majority are struck dumb when asked to talk about their own sexuality, that is, sexual likes and dislikes.

Hence it is important at this stage to have some honest talking. The ideal from our point of view is to look to marriage itself as the place for sexual intercourse. This will no doubt to a degree depend upon your value system, so consult the section 'V is for Values' for a fuller discussion on this. At all costs talk through carefully what you are looking for from your sexual/physical relationship. If it simply boils down to self-centred pleasure you will quickly grow tired of your partner and look for ever-increasing amounts of stimulation. However, if it is to give as much as to take pleasure, and to respect the human dignity of your partner, then a full and exciting life lies ahead of you.

It is also important to talk through previous sexual encounters, fears and expectations so that you are communicating and understanding each other in what can prove a more complex area than it at first appeared.

Spiritual relationship. By this we mean those inner aspirations that motivate you. To discover that your fiancé(e) is an entrepreneurial land developer, while you are a major campaigner for Brazilian rain forests, can lead to tension.

It was St Augustine who pointed out that within every individual there is a God-shaped gap. It is what goes in that gap which counts at this level of relationship. Therefore, some honest talking about what and why you believe things is essential. The section 'V is for Values' should also be consulted here.

Again it would appear that such talk of God is somewhat scorned today. However, we all have values which motivate us. If we don't share the same values we will find conflict at times of pressure and perhaps an inability to take clear decisions with which we both agree.

We share a Christian faith which at times of conflict or stress has proved invaluable in finding a way forward. To recognise that there is a God who loves, cares for and originally created us and to grow to know Him personally is a wonderful experience. To be in a position to pray together strengthens the marriage. To read the Bible and discover a common value system is marvellous.

A successful marriage will enjoy a shared spiritual base. If you want to know more about how we have worked this out we would be pleased to send you a copy of our book *Praying Together*. This gives details of developing a spiritual life together, costs £3.25, including postage and packing, and is available from the publisher's address at the back of this chapter.

Expectations of marriage

This period of engagement is also a time when you should personally identify your expectations of marriage and as ever talk them through with your betrothed. By 'expectations' we mean what your ideal for your marriage is and what you will therefore be looking for.

Each of you take a moment now to jot down your expectations. Then compare notes. You should consider how you anticipate beginning and ending each day (one of Katey's expectations was that we would always retire to bed together), the level of support you expect in your job from your partner, how you envisage running the home (chores, shopping, etc) and the amount of time spent together and apart.

Some years after we married we discovered that we had both entered marriage with low expectations of success and enduring happiness. We only discovered this when talking it through unexpectedly one day during a conversation as to how surprised we were at the level of happiness we had from being married to each other.

There are basically three types of marriage to aim at.

The first is a marriage of *minimum involvement*. This is common today in our culture; especially where both partners are pursuing careers outside the home. Such a relationship makes few demands and hence there are few expectations to fulfil. It is a perfectly adequate form of marriage so long as both partners are in agreement. The danger comes when changes occur in circumstances, for example with the arrival of the first child, and one partner is no longer working full time outside the home and feels a sense of loss of social contact and mental stimulation.

Therefore, in such a marriage, beware the impact of changing circumstances and take the necessary preparatory steps to embrace them.

The second is a marriage of *maximum involvement*. This is the favourite option for idealistic couples. It involves a decision by the couple to share their lives together as completely as possible. Equal value and status are attached to the personal and vocational needs of each other. The interpersonal relationship between the couple is the greatest objective for this type of marriage.

To sustain such a relationship, a high price has to be paid. Our culture does not favour it and it has been estimated that only 5-10% of couples achieve this type of marriage.

The final is a marriage of *measured involvement*. This is a more realistic goal and we highly recommend it. In this type of marriage a high level of individual freedom is maintained while enjoying a reasonable amount of togetherness. It gives marriage a worthy place among the couple's commitments but does not award it an unrealistic priority.

Consider what you intend to aim at as a couple. Ask yourselves the following two questions:

1. What are we aiming at?
2. What framework will we establish to redefine our aims as our marriage matures and circumstances change?

It cannot be stressed too strongly that establishing an effective process for discussing where each of you feel the marriage is at, and to take stock of the potential impact of changes in circumstances, is essential for ensuring that a marriage will grow ever stronger and both partners feel fulfilled and active participants.

Finally, it is worth remembering that you will need to talk through the wedding day together. It is *your* wedding. Parental desires may need to be considered seriously but your own preferences are paramount. Think about and discuss your personal aspirations for the day. This may include constructive conversations with parents but aim to include the elements that will make the day special for you both and a day worth remembering. See 'W is for Wedding Day' for further comments on this.

Praying Together is available in bookshops or from Kingsway Publications, 1 St. Anne's Road, Eastbourne, East Sussex BN21 3UN.

is for Finance

'INSTANT CREDIT!' 'BUY NOW; pay later!' 'Increase your spending power now!' These and similar messages greet us in high street windows, magazines, newspapers and TV commercials. And yet the sad truth behind such statements is that there is no such thing as free money. You pay for everything you purchase; sometimes at a price you never imagined and certainly cannot afford.

Today many young couples are languishing under an intolerable burden of debt which they see very little opportunity of paying off. The consequences are tension, stress and, unfortunately, marriage breakdown.

Why is it that so many difficulties arise concerning the household finances?

As we prepare many young couples for marriage, most are carrying a level of debt into their marriage with them from day one. This is often in the form of outstanding credit card debt (Visa, Access, etc), monies owed on storecards (Next, Benetton and the like) or bank loans taken out for that irresistible sound system or some form of 'wheels'.

All of us need to recognise that there is great pressure to purchase a vast range of so-called 'essential' goods in society today. The advertisers are dedicated to ensuring that their clients outsell their competitors; and sell to *you*. Everywhere we turn there are appealing pictures with the hidden message that we are somewhat incomplete or second class if we are not the proud owners of whatever is depicted.

This is where the problem begins: other people convincing us of what we need. You will no doubt have discovered already just how many people are interested in your wedding. They try to sell you this outfit, those floral arrangements, that honeymoon package. Usually each item is just slightly beyond what you said you would like to spend. Yet it does look so lovely and, after all, it is only *just* beyond what you were thinking of spending.

Then of course there is the argument, presented with a real smooth and sentimental tone: 'Well, you only get married once and it is a very special occasion for you both,' as though such reasoning will of itself add money to your bank account which is currently groaning under the weight and number of demands already being placed upon it.

Of course they say that love is blind and at times the whole momentum that builds up around the wedding preparations can generate a false sense of security. We lose touch with reality. Although we can't afford, we spend. Our concentration is entirely focused on the wedding day, with little thought for the months and years beyond. Beware, for this is a trap which every couple should resist falling into.

It is not that such luxuries are somehow evil. But in the early years of marriage particularly, income levels can be stretched. Furthermore, it is easy to forget that alongside the special purchase of luxuries there are the ongoing costs for heating, lighting, telephone, etc. So often a couple's plans are thrown out by the arrival of the quarterly gas bill which had been left out of the financial computations.

What is credit?

Very simply, credit is a way of enjoying goods or services before we have paid for them. The most obvious illustration in the UK is a mortgage, where a building society or bank advances the capital sum required to purchase a house, and you, the mortgagee, agree to pay a set sum each month for a period of, on average, twenty-five years. Hence you enjoy the benefit of what is called 'a home of your own' but at the discretion of the lender.

In return for this financial service, and the opportunity to occupy your own house, you pay a rate of interest for the money borrowed. This rate is referred to as the mortgage rate and represents how much in real terms the house is costing you.

For example, you purchase a £40,000 house and borrow £30,000 to do so. If the mortgage rate stayed at 12% you would in fact pay £159,000 over twenty-five years for your £30,000. Obviously, however, mortgage rates vary so it is never quite as simple as this illustration but the point is made. It costs money to borrow money. Credit can be very expensive. (See 'M is for Mortgage' for more on the subject of house purchase and house rental.)

The reason why so many people purchase their accommodation by means of a mortgage is that property generally tends to appreciate in value. It is what one calls an appreciating asset. Unfortunately, the majority of goods (cars, furniture, electrical equipment) are depreciating assets. They lose their value over a period of time and in times of financial difficulty you are unable to sell for anything like their original value, let alone with the cost of borrowed money added as well. A house, however, can usually be sold and provide sufficient finance to pay off the lender (eg building society) and hence leave no outstanding debts.

Therefore 'credit' is really a polite way of describing debt. Of course, no one wants to consider themselves in debt, so calling credit cards 'debt cards' would not make commercial sense. Hence the adoption of the user-friendly term 'credit'. It's amazing what difference a word can make.

Let Mike illustrate. He travels widely with his work. As a result he needs to purchase railway tickets, petrol and airline tickets regularly. The simplest way to do so is by means of a credit card. However, having made his purchases he is not in credit to British Rail, but in fact in debt to them. If he doesn't clear his credit card account by the due date he incurs interest charges, so begins to pay extra for the services he has already used. Working with an expense account from his employer he is in a position to cover the monthly accounts on time, so it is a useful and convenient way for him to organise his business finance.

So why do people pay by credit?

Obviously the advertisers are at work to convince us that we need things we as yet don't possess. Never underestimate the desire to own. It can remove all rational argument at times.

It is also a very convenient way of paying. Passing over a credit card is far more painless than parting with cash or even a cheque. It should also allow you to spread your payments to match your cashflow, although you must exercise good discipline at this point for such an argument to prove valid.

In recent years, those offering credit have also tried to link possession of their credit card with a sense of being a cut above the rest of society; attaching status to card ownership and offering a short cut to improving your self-image.

Finally, an offer of a small financial contribution to

your favourite, environmentally friendly charity each time you use their card is the latest inducement to encourage people to adopt credit as a way of life.

If you can see beyond the marketing, and with a clear head consider what is really convenient to your household's budget, then you will handle the credit question very well.

One final point here. You will need to distinguish between fixed term and revolving credit. For fixed term credit you will be told as you make the agreement what the repayments will be and when you are to make them. These will in fact vary slightly because of changes in the Annual Percentage Rate (APR) (see below).

Revolving credit is what most store and all bank credit cards and charge cards offer. In brief, a fixed credit limit is set for the cardholder and interest is charged at the end of each month on the outstanding credit. However, the interest charged at the end of month one is added to the credit outstanding figure and contributes to the amount of interest charged at the end of month two and thence subsequent monthly accounts.

With revolving credit the danger is that the amount outstanding is so large that the interest grows at a faster rate than the repayments. You cannot escape from your indebtedness.

Where does credit come from?

There are four major sources from which credit can be obtained: finance companies, banks, credit cards and stores. It would be worth considering from which of the above sources you enjoy credit. Also, jot down the amounts owed so that you get a picture of your indebtedness; how much you owe.

A fifth source of credit is the mail order catalogue which a large number of folk use to purchase items of clothing, etc, from the comfort of their own front room.

Generally, payment is made by putting a small sum down and then paying regular amounts on a monthly or weekly basis. It is worth noting in passing that items purchased in this way are often more expensive than when bought directly from the shops.

When we consider the four major sources of credit we also discover that storecards are underwritten by finance companies' schemes and that the banks issue credit cards, eg Visa, Access.

Whenever you are considering credit remember three key points:

One: You are committing yourself to spend as yet unearned money.

Two: You are most likely to be purchasing luxury items, not everyday essentials.

Three: Borrowing money is expensive: the retail price plus the interest charges, which increase the longer the period you elect to pay over.

The cost of credit

As we have pointed out, nothing is free in this life. Credit costs. To find out how much it will cost, you will need to do a number of small sums each time you consider a credit purchase.

First, you will encounter the letters APR. These letters stand for the Annual Percentage Rate. Government demands that anyone offering credit must inform the customer what the APR is. And this provides you with the real cost of the goods you anticipate buying on credit.

If you are intimidated by mathematics, as we are (Mike still counts using his fingers!), you should ask the retailer to compute the APR for you. If he won't, purchase elsewhere.

In simple terms, the higher the APR figure the higher the amount of interest. Also, the shorter the period of the loan the cheaper it will be, even though the monthly payments on a long term loan are apparently so much smaller.

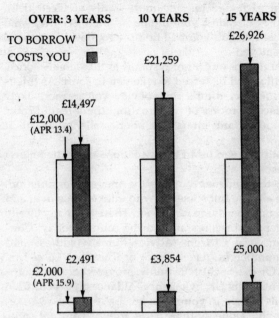

DIAGRAM 1: CREDIT AND DEBIT

OVER: 3 YEARS   **10 YEARS**   **15 YEARS**

TO BORROW ☐
COSTS YOU ▨

£26,926

£21,259

£14,497

£12,000
(APR 13.4)

£2,491   £3,854   £5,000

£2,000
(APR 15.9)

Consequences of credit

If you fail to make your credit payments you become what is known as a 'defaulter'; that is, you have defaulted on your commitment to pay. You will receive a *default notice* terminating your agreement, usually within seven days. The lender or creditor demands full and immediate payment on the outstanding sum and will charge *default interest* on whatever isn't repaid.

Furthermore, he is entitled to repossess goods if you have them on a hire purchase agreement. Or, if you had taken out a secured loan, he can take what security you had agreed in order to get his money back. Beware the small print on any loan agreement, especially those wonderful newspaper ads offering to pay off all your existing debts in exchange for one more easily serviced debt. Often they demand your home as their security, and should you default you will find the roof over your head being removed.

If you do not or cannot respond to the default notice, the creditor will be forced to take you to court. As this is risky from the creditor's point of view you are more likely first to face a process of intimidation: the threat of court action, unpleasant letters and phone calls, often late at night.

Should you end up in this situation, apply the following rules:

First, tell someone outside the immediate situation. Not just anyone but someone who understands debt and will listen with a sympathetic ear. There are many locally based debt counsellors around the country today. Contact your local Citizens Advice Bureau (address and phone number in *Yellow Pages* or *Thomsons Local Directory*). Or many churches now provide help and support. Contact the UK Evangelical Alliance on 071 582 0228 for details of help in your area.

Secondly, alone with a close friend, confront your desire for purchasing all the luxuries. What is it that really affords you fulfilment and satisfaction in life? If you can break from finding your identity in what you possess, and cease comparing yourself with those around you and what they own, you will have taken a major step forward in avoiding further or future debt.

is for Groom

THE GROOM OR BRIDEGROOM is so called because his is the privilege of attending to the bride—for the rest of their lives together. Indeed, the wedding day really is the first day of the rest of your lives.

Compared with the bride's responsibilities the groom gets away pretty lightly. His specific tasks are as follows:

1. Choosing a best man or groomsman
2. Selecting ushers
3. Selecting and booking the honeymoon
4. Purchasing the wedding rings
5. Tipping where appropriate
6. Organising the departure from the wedding reception

Use the above checklist as a guide as you make all the necessary arrangements for your wedding. The specific responsibilities are outlined below.

Choosing a best man

Obviously the groom will want to select someone trustworthy to fulfil this essential task. The answer to a smooth running occasion and a stress free groom is a competent best man.

When Mike played this role first time around, on arrival at the hotel for the reception he made immediate contact with the maitre d'hotel. Requesting details of who would be making announcements and guiding the guests to their places, and who would be announcing the arrival of the bride and groom, he was surprised to learn that it was all down to him.

This entailed maintaining a watchful eye on the photographs in the hotel grounds so that on their cessation he could move the guests through to the wedding breakfast. All went well until he requested the gathering to be upstanding to receive the bride and groom, and the door opened to reveal the bride's brother returning from a comfort break.

A secure, responsible individual is indispensable since they may well have to problem solve on the run without alarming the immediate family nor enabling the guests to spot anything is out of place.

Quite frequently the groom may request his brother to fulfil the role of best man. Alternatively, it could be a good friend of long standing. It is a good idea to let your future bride know your proposed choice of best man ahead of time to get her perspective. It is worth bearing in mind that although the wedding is only one day, the marriage extends for quite a few years beyond that. To select a best man who is a good friend and who will continue to build a relationship with you and your wife over the years following is a good idea.

Mike chose a college friend to act as best man. Although we now live in different parts of the UK we keep in contact and the friendship is such that we can take up from where we left off whenever we meet up. We have also taken an ongoing interest in what the other is doing.

Once the best man is chosen, an informal invitation,

eg a phone call, should be extended. This should be done a good few months before the wedding in case he declines or is unavailable. Believe it or not some grooms don't get around to finding someone until a few days before the wedding. This is unhelpful as it leaves the groom carrying all the responsibilities for the wedding.

It is important to ensure that the best man is available on the day before the wedding ceremony. He is the means by which the groom guarantees to retain his sanity and is assured of a spare pair of legs to run around looking after him.

The best man is responsible for organising the stag party (more of which below). However, his main responsibility throughout is to attend to the needs of the groom. Therefore, ensure he is fully briefed on the day's arrangements. A visit to the reception location and an introduction to the manager can prove most helpful. Also, a conversation with the bride's parents will reassure them that you have selected a reliable individual. Hopefully they will like him as well.

If the wedding is a formal occasion and morning suits are to be hired then the best man should accompany you to Moss Bros (or similar hirer) and take responsibility for returning hire clothes afterwards. If it is less formal, then it is a good idea to invite your best man to accompany you when you go to purchase your wedding outfit. It is increasingly fashionable to match in some way, by sporting the same tie for example.

Of course the budget may not extend to purchasing. This does not matter. Hiring does work out very reasonably at around £40.00 for the weekend. Suits can be picked up the day before the wedding and returned the next day the shop is open. Alternatively, invest some money in a striking new tie or shirt to give a little extra lift to an existing suit. Or wear a flamboyant buttonhole. Of course, you could be completely radical and adopt jeans and a T-shirt but check the disposition of the bride's mother first! You could set off on entirely the wrong foot with your future in-laws.

Once the day of the wedding arrives the best man becomes indispensable. It is he who dashes out to purchase anything that you have neglected, such as cufflinks for that shirt you hired with the morning suit. When your fingers refuse to work as you get dressed it is he who secures your shirt buttons. He also protects you from unexpected and/or unwelcome visitors.

If the wedding is in the afternoon it is customary for the best man to organise a light lunch for the groom in a suitable, pleasant location. This is essential if the reception is late in the day and there is a danger of the groom passing out during the service through the deadly mixture of hunger, heat and excitement. An invitation to the groom's parents to join the lunch party is most acceptable.

Selecting ushers

Apart from the best man the groom must ensure that the ceremony itself is well stewarded. Obviously a registry office requires nothing in comparison with Winchester Cathedral. So the issue is wholly dependent upon the type of ceremony selected.

The tasks that need to be covered are:

1. Handing out orders of service
2. Escorting guests to their seats
3. Answering guests' questions
4. Directing guests for the photographs
5. Ensuring guests find their way to the reception
6. Meeting the needs of the wedding party

The ushers are usually friends or relatives of the groom. They operate under instruction from the best man. The best of ushers have the capacity to use their initiative, having been clearly briefed by the best man.

Their duties do not cease until the last of the guests have left the reception.

The importance of good ushers becomes clear once the wedding ceremony begins since both groom and best man are fully involved and cannot deal with anything apart from the business of the marriage service.

Selecting and booking the honeymoon

Consult the section headed 'H is for Honeymoon' for further, detailed information. Suffice to say here that it is the groom who must ensure all honeymoon arrangements are made.

This involves confirming bookings, collecting tickets, organising passports and valid visas where appropriate, and organising foreign currency and traveller's cheques and checking on arrangements to and from airports if relevant.

The one golden rule which cannot be stressed enough is make sure you book your honeymoon well in advance.

Purchasing the wedding rings

Before you can buy your intended her wedding ring you first have to find out what her preference is. If she has an engagement ring the wedding ring should complement it. It should be of the same material and, if gold, the same carat. She will have very set views no doubt on whether it is to be plain or patterned, thick or thin and various other aspects. Never did buying a ring appear so complex. It will also need to fit her finger and hopefully you will remember the size from purchasing the engagement ring.

Today, most fiancées accompany their bridegroom to be to purchase the ring so that a number can be tried on to see how they sit alongside the existing engagement ring.

Although gold is expensive, if you are prepared to

shop around a good deal should be found. Sometimes you will find a high street jeweller who will give you a discount if you purchase the engagement and wedding rings from the same store. Also, it is well worth while considering second hand purchase.

Finally, it will need to be decided whether the groom will also wear a wedding ring. This is becoming a very common practice today.

Both rings are entrusted to the best man on the day of the wedding and he produces them when asked to by the person officiating at the wedding ceremony.

Tipping where appropriate

It is essential to establish before the wedding if the chauffeur, for example, will expect a small tip. Mike well remembers one wedding when the groom pushed some money into his hand and said in a stage whisper, 'Go tip the driver.' If there are such tasks, equip the best man with the necessary funds and instruct him to act as appropriate.

Organising the departure from the wedding reception

Very simply, this is the area where the groom needs to prepare carefully in advance. If you are leaving a disco late at night to travel to your honeymoon hotel for a romantic first night together as Mr and Mrs, then you do not want the car so impaired that you need to stop and clean it off within a mile of leaving the waving hordes whom you imagined were your friends until you saw the vehicle.

Make sure your best man knows when you intend to leave the reception and on the day give him a half hour warning. Also, ensure that he is in charge of the car decorating ceremony. Give clear instructions as to what is and what is not permissible; this will test his leadership skills.

The greatest danger is of people tampering with your luggage, so take steps to protect yours and your wife's. Having changed into going away outfits entrust any baggage to your best man to organise taking to the car.

At the time of departure steer your wife on your arm through the revellers to both sets of parents to say farewell. Escort your bride to the car and open the door for her, ensuring she is comfortably ensconced before shutting the door. You might have prewarned her to lock it as soon as it is closed! Then get in yourself and drive off—carefully.

The stag party

This is traditionally the bachelor's last fling of freedom before entering the shackles of marriage. Fortunately, in these days of sexual equality, such sexist perspectives are disappearing. However, the idea of a night of celebration with one's male friends is still worth indulging in.

The arrangements are the responsibility of the best man. A short list of the groom's friends should be drawn up. This should also include brothers of the bride, if appropriate. The tradition of only unmarried males being eligible has largely disappeared, although women are still regarded as most inappropriate.

Invitations are informal and made by means of a phone call most conveniently. The location should preferably have a private room for such an occasion to prevent boisterous behaviour annoying other diners. The proprietor should also be informed that the booking is for a stag party. Some establishments may refuse you on that basis and it is better to arrive to a friendly welcome if the evening is to prove successful.

The cost per head is a most important item as it may limit peoples ability to attend. Since the objective is fun and frivolity, then a gourmet meal is probably unnecessary. Many restaurants are prepared to provide a set meal for a reasonable price which means the party members are aware of their costs ahead of time. It is the best man's responsibility to organise the collection of the money and payment of the bill.

Obviously the cost of the groom's meal is met by the others. After all, this is their send off to him. However, the groom may like to buy a round of pre-prandial drinks as people arrive. Indeed, the groom should ensure he is first to arrive in order to welcome his friends. He can leave the best man to worry about the practical details throughout the evening.

It is also traditional for a couple of brief speeches to be made. The first, by the best man, is to say a few words of fond farewell to the groom as he leaves bachelordom and enters the ranks of the married. It may include references to unusual and embarrassing events in the groom's life and should be humorous but never unkind.

The groom then responds, acknowledging his changing state, requesting financial assistance and doing all with a humorous air.

It is then quite appropriate for two or three other contributions from the floor. These should again be short yet amusing.

Following the conclusion of the meal the party carries off the groom to carry out some awful rite of initiation of their own choosing. Stories of grooms placed on ferries to the continent or having legs put in plaster are hopefully more apocryphal than real. However, they illustrate what should *not* be done. A bit of fun, such as a dunk in the sea or a frozen trout down the trousers, brings the stag night to a satisfactory conclusion.

The reception speech

Briefly and finally, the groom does have the privilege of making a speech at the reception. This is a nerve-wracking experience for those unused to speechmaking. However, a bit of thought ahead of the occasion can spare a lot of nervous tension.

Of the three speeches traditionally made (bride's father, bridegroom and best man) the groom's is second, following the bride's father. He is introduced by the best man.

The areas normally covered in what should be a short speech are:

1. Thanks to parents
2. Appreciation for in-laws
3. The story of how the couple met
4. Some affirmation and compliments to the bride
5. Thanks to the best man
6. A comment on the beauty of the bridesmaids
7. A toast to the bridesmaids

You don't have to be humorous. The best advice is to prepare something before the reception, stick to it and be yourself. Surprisingly, when we are true to ourselves people take to us much more easily and the speech is not an ordeal. The time honoured wisdom of 'Stand up, speak up and shut up' is worth paying heed to. In other words, make sure you can be seen by all, heard by all and are sufficiently brief so as not to bore all!

You are now set up to prove a most effective bridegroom.

H

is for Honeymoon

ORIGINALLY 'HONEYMOON' REFERRED to the first month after marriage. Now it is used to describe the holiday taken by the newly-married couple immediately after their wedding. However, if both partners hold active and demanding jobs, a holiday proper may be delayed until some mutually convenient time in the not-too-distant future, and this again will be described as the honeymoon.

Some of you may feel it's a shame that employers are not sufficiently enlightened to restore the word to its true meaning and grant a full month off after the wedding. With the wedding day itself completed one could be forgiven for thinking that a month was not really sufficient time to recover one's energy and emotional stability after the manic attentions of parents, in-laws and assorted relatives. The stress of 'the big day' has to be experienced to be believed!

The honeymoon, therefore, is a first-class opportunity to rest and recover, as well as the start of a lifetime's commitment to each other.

Where to go

This depends on the state of your pocket and each partner's preference. Let's begin with the pocket, or the cost of the honeymoon.

Basically the sky is the limit. As you prepare for your wedding you will no doubt discover that you are very popular. You read magazines on marriage, largely filled with advertisements of what the happy couple will seek to furnish their home with. Likewise, the department store(s) handling the wedding list will also shower you with splendid magazines highlighting all the material resources the 'normal' couple require in setting out on their marriage. Hence you become prime targets for those selling holidays: '...champagne awaiting you in the bed-room, corner bath, revolving bed, eighteen course "morning after!!" breakfast', etc.

Weddings are expensive. You have also probably just undertaken a mortgage and it is only the excitement of the wedding which has prevented you from acknowledging its crippling effects. There *is* life after the honeymoon, and life that will involve expenditure. The first question therefore is: What can you afford?

Decisions on honeymoons can be taken, and are advisably taken, nine to twelve months before the wedding. This means there is no last minute rush and plenty of time to secure what you want and not settle for anything that is left. This also gives you time to save something for the cost both of the honeymoon and spending money while away.

It is at this point that you need to settle on your preference. One may like the Lake District, the other the Greek Islands. While traditionally it is the groom's responsibility to organise and pay for the honeymoon, in these enlightened days it is constructive to do some detective work, ie have a conversation about preferences. If the bride in question has a phobia about flying, take it into consideration. Such a conversation does not prevent

61

the setting up of a surprise honeymoon but does save the awful sense of disappointment with all the related stress that brings to the relationship.

Organising the honeymoon

Having determined to what part of the world you are going, and having set a budget which you can afford and which the most persuasive travel agent will not be able to push you beyond (even though he is armed with a case of free wine and six free entry competitions promising 'the lucky winners' time share for life), you are ready to start searching.

Begin by taking advice from friends. They may have discovered the ideal honeymoon island. They should be able to direct you to a good travel agent. Remember, this is your honeymoon, so however inferior you feel stepping through the doors of the travel agents you are the customer and the customer is always right.

Decisions do not have to be made on the spot, and indeed are best not made then. Take away brochures. Ask about any little extras that will make it special for you. It does pay to let the hotel know you are a honeymoon couple, however embarrassed you may feel, since you will often benefit from special treatment. Mike well remembers discovering our hotel room filled with fresh flowers which were a delight. What's more, Katey gave him all the credit which he gladly received. It's only now she's discovered the truth!

Enquire whether your hotel is surrounded by discos that will blare out music all night so that you can avoid these if you want to. It is often a good idea to write out a list of questions before you go so that your mind doesn't go blank in the middle of a discussion with the travel agent.

Remember you will be tired. The week preceding the wedding and the day itself are demanding, physically and emotionally. Therefore organise flights sensibly. The last thing you want is to be sitting in an airport lounge at 1.00am waiting for your 'discount' flight.

By planning ahead you may choose to spend the first night at a hotel near the airport of departure or a few miles into your journey if staying in Britain. This means you have the minimum of hassle once you have got away from the celebrations, especially sensible if you will be having a disco or evening party following the reception for all those friends you were unable to invite. *The honeymoon is for your benefit so plan accordingly.*

If you are planning to honeymoon in UK, then visit the reference section of your local library. They have all the hotel, Bed & Breakfast, camping and such guides. They can also give you a pen and paper to take notes. With your preferences in mind, study the relevant key page explaining the symbols used throughout the guide. This is essential when pricing each lodging. You can find good deals to suit your pocket and meet your criteria (from city to rural isolation).

Once you have made a selection, phone the proprietor to check the guide's details remain as read, and place a provisional booking which should be followed up with a written confirmation. This can increasingly be faxed through in most cases today.

Preparing for the honeymoon

If you are travelling abroad do check with your GP or health centre nurse whether vaccinations are required. You will often need to begin these eight weeks before departure. Sometimes vaccine will need to be ordered so get organised early.

Passports are also essential for the world traveller. We know of one couple who missed their honeymoon when a helpful official *at the airport* pointed out that one of the passports was out of date. Imagine their disappointment.

We also know of a couple who successfully completed their honeymoon only discovering on their return home that one passport was beyond its expiry date. Two cases known to us, so it does happen. Check dates and details now.

Also, if you are applying for your first passport or a renewal do leave plenty of time. Bureaucracy can move exceedingly slowly and never appears to recognise special cases, however hard you argue. It is worth noting that the woman can apply for a passport in her married name before the wedding.

Many banks or travel agents require you to order foreign currency several days in advance. Work out how much you want to carry. It's convenient to carry large amounts in the form of traveller's cheques. Banks and building societies will issue these and you will need your passport with you when collecting them. The advantage of traveller's cheques is that they can be cancelled if stolen, saving you from losing your holiday money. Once abroad you can cash them at banks and many shops; always keep an eye out for the best rate of exchange and check if there is a service charge involved (usually a percentage of the amount you are changing).

It is worth talking with others who have visited your chosen romantic location to find out if it is better to carry sterling, as the exchange rate may well be in your favour within the country rather than 'cashing up' before leaving Britain.

If heading for sunny climes remember sun tan lotion, sunglasses and something for upset stomachs and headaches (the real and not the excuse type!). If remaining in Britain take suitable clothing for the unpredictable weather.

On arrival

Check into your hotel or pick up the keys to your self-catering cottage or apartment, and ensure that what you ordered or were told would be there is there. If not, summon up the courage to mention anything you are unhappy about to the reception desk or equivalent. Remember, you have paid your money so ensure you get what you have paid for. Don't just moan and complain to each other in the standard British way.

If in a hotel discover where the dining room is, how room service works (and what charges are applied when you order via room service), where the swimming pool is and what time it opens. Check meal times, morning tea/coffee, etc. If hungry on arrival order a meal.

If abroad make enquiries for maps, public transport arrangements, hiring cars, cost of taxis, etc. These details will help you to become acclimatised very quickly. Look through tours on offer or places of interest worth visiting and talk through a schedule for your honeymoon. It's good to provide some definition as to how time is to be spent; if you are both sun worshippers and there's an abundance of sun then you won't require any other diversions.

Obviously the honeymoon is about making love together; beginning a physical partnership which is akin to a journey. Over the years you will discover more about each other and what pleases your partner, and you will become increasingly expert and confident in the art of sex. (Read 'S is for Sex' for further information on this essential topic.)

The honeymoon should be the time for laying an initial foundation to your marriage. Whatever else was true about your relationship before your wedding, it was not a marriage. Now you have publicly committed yourselves to each other for life and need gently to build a strong relationship. Don't rush—you have a lifetime ahead of you. This is the start of the greatest adventure of your lives!

Honeymoon disasters

Now, for your encouragement, everything is not guaranteed to go right as you depart on your honeymoon. So if you have a disaster, don't panic; chalk it up to experience.

One couple, having left their reception, were looking forward to disappearing off to some far flung overseas location. On arriving at the airport all flights were fog bound so they spent their first night in the departure lounge. Perhaps not the most auspicious location for the first night of your honeymoon.

Another couple we know arrived safely at their destination and, having consummated the marriage, fell fast asleep only to wake with a scream when their bottoms touched in bed.

Yet another couple had the difficult task of explaining to the hotel how it was they had come to break their bed.

Perhaps the most awful experience belonged to the couple who were distressed to hear the hotel fire alarms go off five minutes after consummating their marriage. That really is a poser; do you trust it is a false alarm or do you evacuate your room?

As for us, we arrived at our hotel. Katey had a temperature of over 100° and went to bed. Mike ordered a large meal courtesy of room service and watched TV. I don't think the porter could quite believe his eyes when he entered the honeymoon suite!

J

is for
Insurance

THIS MAY SEEM a strange heading to come across in a book on preparing for marriage. Yet very soon you are going to commit yourself to someone else's welfare, 'for better for worse, for richer for poorer, in sickness and in health'. These are significant promises and commitments to make.

Of course when we marry we basically believe it's for better, richer and health. Naturally we don't assume it is for calamity. If we did we wouldn't get married in the first place. However, it is important that we think through carefully what financial provision and protection we are to invest in as a precaution against future difficulties.

There is nothing worse than being struck by sudden unemployment or having your residence burgled and discovering there is no means of meeting the financial consequences of such events.

No doubt you will have read all sorts of newspaper ads offering everything from car insurance to life assurance. Alternatively, you may have been canvassed by phone or at your door by enthusiastic and persuasive salespersons seeking to sign you up for a policy of one sort or another. Since their income depends a great deal on commissions paid out by companies on policies they have sold, it is little wonder they are so pushy.

So where do you turn to for advice? Open up your *Yellow Pages* or equivalent and turn to 'Financial Services'. You will find a list of financial advisers. You will then seek out a suitable adviser who meets certain important criteria.

First, you will want to ensure that they display a logo that tells you they are 'A FIMBRA Member'. FIMBRA is a regulatory body which everyone who wishes to offer financial advice on life assurance, pensions, investment, etc, must be registered with. The qualifications for membership are: relevant experience and a well run, financially sound and efficient business. These ground rules have been laid down by the Financial Services Act.

Secondly, you need to check that they are operating as an independent financial adviser. If they are, they will

display the IFAP logo. Such an adviser is obliged by law to research the relevant policies offered by different companies and then advise you on the most beneficial course of action for your circumstances.

If you make an approach direct to a specific company, or take the advice of a broker who may be operating an agency for a certain firm, such an individual may only be operating such an agency on a part-time basis as a means of generating extra income. Alternatively, at worst they may in fact be no more than a 'cowboy' whose advice is hardly worth the paper it is written on.

It is also worth stating that if you are self-employed then the whole question of insurance is one you should get advice on as you are in a vulnerable position if you find yourself unable to work at any stage.

When it comes to insurance there are basically two types: insurance of yourself and insurance of your possessions. We are usually better acquainted with the second type.

Insurance of yourself

1. Life assurance. This, as its name suggests, is an insurance payable in the event of your death. At present, death is probably the last thought going through your mind; and quite rightly. However, it is advisable to consider the circumstances in which your partner will be left should you die. Initially, with you both earning, the only consideration may be the outstanding mortgage. You were no doubt offered a mortgage protection scheme to cover this eventuality. Basically the insurance is to pay off the mortgage in the event of the death of one of the named owners. This means no more mortgage payments and a chance to take stock. Most building societies and banks include it as part of the package. However, you don't need to take the package they offer and can seek independent financial advice for the best deal. You do not need a mortgage to take out life assurance. Most couples think more seriously about it once children arrive. If one partner were to die the sum payable would contribute towards maintaining the children, especially as one parent finds it hard to act as breadwinner as well as look after the kids. In order to obtain life assurance you will be expected to fill out long and detailed forms. All serious illnesses or existing health problems will have to be declared. Failure to do so may nullify the policy and prevent payment. Also, height and weight relationship will have a marked impact upon the premiums, so diet if necessary before you fill out the forms. Finally, the younger you start the cheaper the premiums will be.

2. Pensions. While many firms used to run a variety of pension schemes for their staff, increasingly a measure of flexibility is being introduced to enable individuals to take out their own pension scheme and transfer it with them when they change jobs. You will need to see what pension provision your place of work offers you, if any.

Again, talk of retirement and pensions may seem somewhat irrelevant but not to make some form of financial provision for later years is irresponsible. Many schemes are on offer and expert advice should be sought. With increasing concern about the environment, a growing number of companies are offering environmentally friendly policies. By this they mean they will not invest your monthly contributions in companies that do not meet the criteria they have established. Again, this may not be on your immediate priority list but should concern you both at some point in the not-too-distant future.

3. *Health.* This is of course much more politically sensitive and you may well have very set ideas already. Just to say health plans are available and if you have a measure of disposable income you may want to consider investing in this area. However, be careful to consider the areas of exclusion in any policy you look at.

4. *Credit.* We have looked at the subject of credit under the title 'F is for Finance'. However, you are able to take out insurance to cover your outstanding credit payments should you suddenly lose your job or be unable to work for some reason. This may be the sort of financial provision that makes sense in your circumstances and does mean you are not left heavily in debt if life takes a turn for the worse.

On all these types of insurance there are income tax benefits to be gained and an independent adviser can explain these to you.

Insurance of your possessions

This covers the more everyday aspects of cars and household contents. Suffice to say for such insurance you can shop around the high street or approach an independent broker. Often this will prove to be someone other than the person you have found specialising in life assurance and the like. However, such an individual can easily advise you on who to turn to.

Again, if you go for a mortgage you will probably be offered a household contents insurance deal along with the insurance you have to take out to cover the rebuilding costs of your residence should it be destroyed.

With contents insurance you may get cheaper rates if window locks are fitted or a burglar alarm is in situ. Indeed, some companies insist on these precautions in areas deemed to be high risk as far as break-ins are concerned. Also be sure to check at what value individual items need to be separately insured. When Katey's engagement ring collapsed we claimed the repair on the insurance. A letter informed us that due to its value it was not covered under the basic terms of the policy and should have been separately itemised. Fortunately, the company made an *ex gratia* payment to cover the repair, but we had discovered something new and very important.

In this whole area of insurance the principles are threefold:

1. What is relevant to our situation?
2. When does it become relevant, eg immediate need or next year?
3. How much can we afford?

Do take the budgetary question very seriously. Everything is available for a price, but can we afford to pay the price—regularly?

At all times openly discuss the provision you are making. Ensure that you both understand the policies. This is rather important if at some point one of you is left on your own. And, finally, at all times ensure that you are in full agreement.

is for
Jokes

A BRIEF RESPITE now follows. It is customary that humour is a part of the traditional speeches on the wedding day. In a moment you will find a number of jokes accumulated on our travels which may be of assistance. Mike's favourite when acting as best man is to rise to his feet and begin: 'Ladies and Gentlemen, I wish to begin by congratulating the groom on his wonderful, nay exquisite, choice of (*dramatic pause here*) best man. I know of no one who could do it better.'

The aim of all such humour is to relax people and add interest to the speeches. At a wedding, although you do not want to come over as a professional comedian, whatever your role, there is a requirement to keep an air of informality, indicating a real relationship with the bride and groom on what is their day.

Also, remember that this is not the occasion for either lewd or personal humour. The embarrassment of either bride or groom is totally unacceptable here. Hence try to include one or two funnies, as well as some words of positive affirmation, to send the bride and groom on their way.

A few funnies

'The groom had a distinguished academic career. When a visiting lecturer arrived to speak on the dangers of alcohol, he used a vivid illustration to make his point. He placed a live worm in a glass of water and one in a glass of whisky. At the end of his lecture he drew attention to the two glasses. The worm in the water was still wriggling about; the one in the whisky was stone dead.

'Turning to his audience he said: "What can be learned from this demonstration?"

'The groom, always a keen student, immediately replied, "If you want to avoid worms, drink whisky." '

'The groom is also a master of logic. On one occasion, entering a chemists to purchase some rat poison (college accommodation really is bad these days), the assistant informed him: "I'm sorry, we don't stock it. Why not try Boots?"

'Our intelligent groom replied somewhat bemused: "I want to poison them not kick them to death." '

'The groom is well known for his compassionate nature. His love for animals is perhaps not quite so well known. Travelling on a bus the other day with a baby alligator in his arms the conductor enquired if he was taking it to the zoo.

' "Don't be silly," he replied, "we are going to the cinema. We did the zoo yesterday." '

'The bride and groom have just invested in a new car and called it Daisy. Some days it goes and some days it don't. It's replaced their old car called Connie, short for constipation. It strained and strained and passed nothing.'

'The groom is certainly a man of creativity. He was seen the other day sitting in a train carriage tearing bits of newspaper up, screwing them into small balls and then throwing them out of the window. When asked what he was doing he replied: "It keeps elephants away."

' "But there aren't any elephants," his companion replied.

' "I know,' the groom responded, "It's very effective isn't it?" '

These can all be chopped and changed around with suitable comments addressed to the bride to the effect that does she really know what she has taken on board?

With one good funny well prepared, whether you are best man, groom or bride's father, you can survive the speech ordeal and come out with flying colours. Just remember to keep it short.

*is for
Keeping House*

OWNING OR RENTING a property carries with it a number of other responsibilities. Not all of these are that attractive at first glance; cleaning, decorating, gardening to name but a few. Yet these and many other tasks are involved in keeping house effectively. How do the newly-married couple work these issues out?

Priorities

There are a vast array of what might be termed labour saving devices currently on the market. No doubt you have either had these thrust before you in innumerable magazines and handouts designed especially for those preparing for marriage or have dreamily window shopped together through large department stores.

It is also apparent that most newly-married couples carry with them the assumption that they will begin life together at the same material point that their parents have currently attained. It may come as some surprise but parents have had quite a number of years working, earning and saving to arrive at their present financial state. Furthermore, with children beginning to spread their 'independence wings' and leave the family nest, parental overheads are diminishing—and not before time many a loving parent would gladly sigh!

As newly weds you need to establish what your disposable income is going to be; not what it might become but what it is now (see 'D is for Daily Budget'). You may well have been given many useful household items as wedding gifts (See 'W is for Wedding Day'), but you will certainly still require certain tools to enable you to keep house effectively, efficiently and conveniently.

When we were married we received £100.00 worth of gifts among our wedding presents. With Katey teaching full time, as well as Mike working in a job which entailed travelling away from home, we decided to invest the money in an automatic washing machine. This meant great excitement for Katey who came from a home where all washing had been done by hand! Indeed in our discussions it was Katey's persuasive logic that carried the day, pointing out as she did that such a labour saving device would ease our life considerably; Mike arriving home with luggage full of dirty washing and in need of an instant turnaround; Katey exhausted from teaching and running a home with three lodgers.

A washing machine was a priority for us. Indeed we got it for exactly £100.00 since we inherited a broken washing machine in the house we purchased which was worth £20.00 in exchange for a new one. It's wonderful what a bit of bartering can achieve.

So what are your priorities? List them individually and then compare lists; it can make for interesting reading and explosive conversation. Having written down your lists and compared them, work out which items are a priority and which a luxury. Luxuries are nice but may not be appropriate if the choice lies between eating an evening meal or steaming in a jacuzzi bath!

Another question worth asking is: Are you able to secure them second hand? A glance through the 'For Sale' ads in the local newspaper or cards in your local news-agent can save you pounds and give you the necessary breathing space to save for its eventual replacement with something of your choice. We were very grateful for the gift of a reconditioned vacuum cleaner which gave sterling service until it was eventually killed off by dog hairs following the purchase of a gorgeous golden retriever puppy. It then took two further vacuum cleaners to discover one that could cope with mounds of dog hair; not because we don't vacuum but because the dog moults a lot.

So don't seek to emulate the parental home immediately. The dishwasher may just have to wait. Do not get taken in by glossy adverts or smooth talking salespeople who infer that you are somehow not quite together if you are not surrounded by the most up-to-the-minute high tech paraphernalia. Rather, spend to your budget, cut corners where you can, ensure you can distinguish between a necessity and a luxury, and relax into being the couple you are and establishing the style of home you both want. The advertisers exist to market and sell. If that involves undermining individuals' self-esteem and self-confidence they will do it. So don't fall prey to their marketing skills. Retain your individuality and make your own choices in line with your budget.

Planning

So what are you most likely to need?

Vacuum cleaner, dusters and floor mop of some suitable type.

Scourer and suitable cloth for washing up. As for tea towels the rather plain 'glass cloths' have proved best value for us. Long lasting and excellent at drying, the shine on glass has to be seen to be believed!

Food processor or equivalent, depending on culinary habits.

A washing machine. A tumble dryer if you are in a flat with no garden or a studio flat (ie the bedroom and lounge are one, and space is therefore at a premium); in other instances we think this is a luxury initially.

Iron and ironing board. Clothes horse (essential throughout the winter months). Outside, we are great advocates of the old-fashioned washing line rather than rotary dryers.

Garden spade, fork, trowel and rake if you have a garden. A mower if you have a lawn, although you may be able to borrow one initially. When purchasing, go for the best mower you can. We tried several of the smaller ones (around £60.00 mark) and found them useless and a lot of hard work. We now have a motor mower which means the grass is cut in fifteen minutes and is therefore no longer the fortnightly chore it once was. The initial outlay was high but the ease of use has more than repaid us for that cost.

The above constitutes the very basic requirements for running a house effectively, efficiently and conveniently. We take it for granted that you will have a cooker and fridge. A freezer is a useful tool if organised and run efficiently; more so if you like to feed off instant convenience foods. A microwave is primarily a tool for dealing with convenience foods from the freezer and is not really an essential part of any house. However we have done away with our traditional cooker and only have a combination microwave which gives us the benefits of microwave and traditional cooking. It also takes up less space in what is a very small kitchen area.

Partnership

It's all very well having the equipment, but who is going to operate it? As yet we are not in the age of the automatic robot, and while servants are making a rapid return you are still very fortunate if you are in the income bracket which enables you to employ such (that is if you agree with the principle in the first place).

There are two routes you may choose to follow.

Route One. You identify the various tasks that need doing and allot each task to husband or wife.

Route Two. Having identified the tasks that need performing regularly, both partners co-operate in an informal way to ensure they are fulfilled.

The second route obviously requires more trust, but does have the benefit of flexibility. If one partner is over-tired, the other can perform tasks without feeling 'hard done by' or unhelpfully self-righteous. Or if one finds they are in from work early then they can get on with sorting the house rather than thinking, 'Well, I've done my tasks so I'll put my feet up and wait for dinner,' only for the other half of the relationship to charge in from work and virtually break his or her neck trying to complete unfinished tasks. This route also enables couples to maximise their free time together since they work for each other in this informal arrangement, and they have more chance of both being able to relax together than when one party still has some tasks remaining.

Success in this area does also depend on one person in the marriage being an organiser; not of their partner but of the tasks that need doing. If neither of you is a natural organiser (you don't salivate when given a Psion or Fil-ofax) then you need to get hold of a small notebook and write down days of the week and allot specific tasks to each day. Then either partner can pick up the book and perform their allotted task (*route one*) or whatever is waiting to be done (*route two*) and mark it off as completed. Believe us, a little organisation saves a multitude of arguments.

Before we set out a hypothetical plan for the week we

want to stress that there are no tasks which are either masculine or feminine. There was a time when gardening was his affair and ironing hers. Fortunately, we now live in more enlightened times and marriage is a partnership jointly owned between husband and wife. Therefore both partners contribute to its success, and performing household tasks is part of the price of a successful marriage. So husbands and wives will have to pay the price if they are to succeed. However, you may dislike certain tasks. This is not wrong, but necessitates honest negotiation. Mike hates ironing and has taken full responsibility for the toilets in order to be relieved from wielding the iron.

Hypothetical weekly task plan

Sunday   Church, relax.
Monday   Grocery shop (usually the quietest night at the supermarket, only check times of closing first).
Tuesday   Vacuum (downstairs only). Dust.
Wednesday Wash (overnight is a good idea and hang out next morning before work).
Thursday   Iron. DIY tasks. Baking for weekend.
Friday   Vacuum whole house and dust ready for weekend. Clean bath, sink and loo.
Saturday   'Top up' shop for weekend. Gardening.

Generate a list to include a plumber, odd-job man, gas engineer, electrician, and any other useful person. Also have a torch, candles and spare fuses easily accessible.

Finally, try to find a local window cleaner to look after the outside windows. There are a number of gadgets on the market promising to make this difficult task easy but they only seem to complicate it further. Support local industry; get a recommended window cleaner (seeking recommendations provides a good way to get to meet your neighbours).

Ten basic helps to keeping a happy house

1. Never put anything down when you can put it away.
2. Always replace the bin liner on emptying the bin.
3. Always replace the loo roll.
4. Keep a running shopping list of items to be replaced in a prominent place (and take it to the shops when you go!).
5. Use the correct tool for the job, ie screwdriver to change plugs not the nearest knife!
6. Put dirty washing in the linen basket—don't use it as an extra decoration to the bedroom.
7. Maintain a stock of spare lightbulbs and fuses in a convenient cupboard.
8. Soak saucepans immediately after use and stack crockery to save kitchen becoming an apparent junk yard.
9. Put cap back on toothpaste after use, clean discarded stubble from sink, clear away hair from plughole after washing and unblock sink or loo if you are the culprit.
10. Apologise to your partner rather than invent an elaborate excuse when you make a mistake or forget to complete some task.

is for Leisure

IT SOUNDS SOMEWHAT inappropriate perhaps to put the question: 'What do you intend to do with your leisure time?' to a couple preparing for marriage. Yet once the novelty of being married has worn off there are quite a number of years ahead with hours to be filled.

Many couples we discover have never discussed their hobbies and interests together. Often such activities appear somewhat irrelevant during the first flush of excitement as the relationship blossoms and then wedding preparations fill every hour of the day and, so it would appear, night! Yet it is often in this area that the cracks and fissures which can lead to break up first appear.

We once had reported to us that a minister preaching from his pulpit used this area to illustrate a somewhat strange and to our minds unhelpful point. Talking on marriage he suggested that in today's 'high tech' society it was exceedingly naive to expect two people to stay together 'till death did them part'. With the increased pace of life people's interests were changing repeatedly through their lives so that the person one married could not be said to be the same person several years on. His conclusion was that we should expect to marry around three different individuals during our adult life; not at the same time of course but following 'amicable' divorces.

Obviously this is not the most wholesome of thoughts to enter marriage with. Certainly we change as the years move on. This is because of experience, circumstances, personal choices and the like. However, with clear communication there is no reason why a marriage should not mature and change along with the two principle characters. Indeed a measure of the quality of the marriage is just such an ability. This demands a commitment to effective communication (see 'P is for Partnership') and an active interest in each other's new and ongoing hobbies.

When we married we did not have much of an idea about each other's leisure interests. Mike was a reader and sportsman; Katey enjoying a strong social life, music and all gregarious activities. This indeed was one of the areas Mike found most difficult since he was not then a particularly sociable character.

Our relationship developed while we were at college. Katey's room was invariably filled with hordes of friends—something which was not to Mike's liking. In fact he felt he needed to book an appointment to have some time with Katey on her own. His reaction was often to get frustrated and moody, and failure to communicate the cause of this frustration did not help Katey to understand his condition nor allow them to talk it through to a suitable resolution. Many hours of non-communication were spent with Mike disappearing to prowl around unhappy, while Katey was trying to analyse what she had done to upset him.

It was only as we learned to discuss together and discover our different interests in life that such unhealthy and time-wasting breakdowns in communication were avoided. As a result Mike confessed his lack of social skills in company hence his insecurity when confronted by a social scene. Katey expressed her lack of interest in reading and sitting for long periods apparently doing nothing, and doing it in silence.

This was important as we entered marriage since Katey insisted that we went to bed at the same time (a practice we continue today), while Mike had to explain that he often liked to read after retiring, which had severe implications for Katey's intended late night witterings! We therefore developed a process where we retired together and Katey would go to sleep after a brief witter, leaving Mike to read. The compromise was that Katey had to learn to sleep with the light on!

These may sound very trite issues but they are the bread-and-butter issues of marriage.

As the years have passed we have discovered interests that we can share together. Mike's first attempts at gaining Katey's interest were fairly high risk and reveal a lot about Mike's lack of diplomacy.

The first occurred while living in Wolverhampton. Celebrating Katey's birthday Mike booked up a meal at a local restaurant. All went well and Katey was delighted with the romantic setting and the thoughtfulness of her partner. Having been promised a further treat after lunch, Katey left the restaurant with a spring in her step and anticipation in her heart. Her excitement turned to horror when she found herself passing through the turnstiles at Molyneaux with the expectation of watching Wolverhampton Wanderers v Norwich. (A soccer match for the uninformed!) Always positive in outlook Katey did appreciate the legs of the players for a full ninety minutes of play!

A similar and second such incident occurred in celebration of one wedding anniversary. Living in Leeds at the time Mike whisked Katey off to Headingly for the day. For those who are not quite sure, this is the home of Yorkshire cricket and also a test match ground. Katey was to have the privilege of seeing the third day's play between England and New Zealand. What had appeared very promising, with a large hamper being loaded into the car, appeared to be turning into a nightmare. However, a strange metamorphosis took place and Katey actually enjoyed the day. Since then she has very much taken to cricket and in this dubious way we discovered a shared interest. Football remains a no go area!

It is advisable to avoid such high risk strategies in discovering shared interests. Not that you will want to do everything together; nor should you. Mike enjoys bird-watching as a hobby. It's not something Katey has any great aspiration to get into. It also affords Mike time and space to himself which he appreciates and needs in order to retain his sanity. So how is it you establish what your and your partner's leisure pursuits are? How do you determine areas of shared interest?

Below is a short questionnaire. Each of you should complete it and then talk through your answers together.

LEISURE QUESTIONNAIRE

1. How many close friends do you have?
2. How often do you see them?
3. Where or in what context do you see them (eg pub, football training)?
4. Does your partner know/like your friends?
5. Will they be welcome in the new home you'll be sharing together?
6. If not, why not?
7. What is your favourite memory from childhood?
8. What were your hobbies as a child?
9. Do you still maintain any of these hobbies? Which ones?
10. Why did you stop them (eg boredom, time factors, grew out of them)?
11. What leisure interests have you now?
12. Does your partner know/share them with you?
13. How do you unwind?
14. Do you enjoy your own company?
15. How do you spend spare time?
16. List in order of preference the following activities:

    (a) Board games
    (b) Reading
    (c) TV
    (d) Videos
    (e) Music—type and bands
    (f) Sport—type and frequency
    (g) Walking
    (h) Theatre
    (i) Gardening
    (j) Other (identify)

17. Where do you like to holiday?
18. What do you like to do on holiday?
19. What would you do with a free evening?
20. Do you have a regular day off each week?

Now you have talked your answers through you will have a far fuller picture of what your partner's leisure interests are. It might also have proved helpful in shedding light on your own pastimes.

It is worth looking at why you finished with some of your childhood hobbies. Obviously we grow up and out of certain activities. (Mike no longer races Corgi cars!) However, sometimes the increased pace of life that usually accompanies teenage years (exams and social life) and then entry into the world of work can squeeze hobbies out.

Mike certainly found this true in his experience. A marvellous teacher called Mr Talents captured Mike's imagination with the world of nature. He remained interested in animal and bird life for most of his childhood. However, as he grew up, partly because it wasn't very 'in' to discuss the mating habits of the badger and partly through lack of time, this interest fell into disrepair. Only in the last few years has he taken up this interest again and found it affords as much pleasure today as it did then.

Sometimes we need to make time to enjoy ourselves. We must all find effective ways to unwind. Often it costs very little to indulge our leisure interests. Increased stress through work and life in general requires that we learn how to rid ourselves of tension and rediscover that life is good on balance, and that we make time to appreciate ourselves as well as each other. The growing incidence of stress-related illnesses, such as ME, indicates that we cannot ignore making time to unwind and relax.

However, it is not always easy to relax. Time on our hands without knowing what to do can lead to pressure and argument. So knowing how we like to relax individually and together helps to ensure that we maximise any leisure time we have. Although it might sound a little contrived, it is important to think about and talk through how to spend free time. Nothing is more frustrating than the feeling that a day together has been frittered away to no purpose. Alternatively, it is equally distressing when one partner is participating in an activity under sufferance, wishing they were doing something else.

So how do we avoid such pitfalls? We always agree how we will spend time off. Imagine that we have a day off together coming up. We know what our interests are, both individual and joint, and so we run through the list to see what grabs us. To illustrate, consider the following list:

Mike's Interests	Katey's interests	Day off activity
Birdwatching	Gardening	Tiredness level
Reading	TV	Weather
Photography	Cooking	Personal space
Walking		Outstanding chores
Cycling	Cycling	Family
Cricket	Cricket	Friends
Historic buildings	Historic buildings	Funds
Public gardens	Public gardens	
Music (classical)	Music (classical)	

Let us concentrate on the final column. These are factors that will enable us to select what we want to do with leisure time.

Tiredness level has a direct bearing on what we feel able to do. If we have been very busy we will not want a long drive. We will probably decide to 'get up slow' as we say. Alternatively, if Katey is tired Mike may opt to get up early and go birdwatching, hence not infringing on time together later.

Weather also has a bearing. A good day suggests a visit to a public garden. A bad day in spring demands a birdwatching trip before breakfast and after tea. Cool but fine may entice us to cycle out for a pub lunch and a cream tea.

Personal space causes us to check how much space we each feel we need to do our own thing. Mike might read for a couple of hours in splendid isolation. Katey may wish to repot a few house plants.

Outstanding chores requires an honest consideration about what ought to have been done around the house from a six-foot lawn and fortnight's ironing to repairing the washing line or installing the smoke alarms.

Family is a check to ensure we haven't ignored parents and assorted kith and kin. We try to make visits to maintain good contact and to keep in touch with all family developments.

Friends often get drawn into our time off. Some enjoy historic houses, others birdwatching or cycling. All enjoy a meal and we often conclude a day off by inviting friends around. It is important to get the balance right between time together and time spent socially. Given what we said above it's worth pointing out that Katey has successfully socialised Mike; a leopard can change his spots with care, craft and a willingness to enrich the marriage relationship.

Funds are often the critical question. A day out without any spending money is a disaster. Every trip needs to be budgeted. It's no good finding that antique light oak bureau on an expedition and either bankrupting yourselves or returning home disappointed, having missed the chance to get something special for the house. Funds have implications affecting whether, when driving any distance, we take sandwiches or plan for lunch out, for example.

Take time to create three similar lists for yourselves. Add your own name and remember to review these lists on, say, an annual basis.

A further area which does require much discussion is holidays. Some like to lay for hours under the sun. Others choose to explore local towns. Yet others struggle with the heat and would prefer Iceland. Additionally, hay fever or some such allergy may prove a factor in choosing locations.

A holiday is for relaxation, rest and recuperation. Therefore both partners must be happy with destination, location and planned activity. Skiing may be wonderful for her but an absolute nightmare for him. Come to a conclusion on what sort of holidays you plan for.

Katey loves to stay at home. If away, she gets bored after a maximum of ten days. We build our holiday plans around these factors. Mike likes to rot and do nothing. That provides another factor. Neither of us likes lazing in the sun; although Mike definitely likes water activities more than Katey does.

If you are an avid skier or yachtperson and your partner does not share your passion then consider taking a week at some point in the year to disappear to indulge your passion. But make sure your spouse has the finance and opportunity to enjoy themselves back home. Perhaps they can visit friends or go on their own special holiday as well.

Be aware of the temptation which can lurk on such solo holidays and don't get caught up in a short-term extra-marital affair. Make sure you maintain some form of contact, either by phone or regular and inventive correspondence.

One final point. With both of us having full-time jobs it is easy to get into diary mismanagement. Katey can invite people who arrive to meet the guests Mike has offered a meal to. This can prove both a source of embarrassment and antagonism. Hence we do seek to get our diaries together on a monthly basis and learn what each other is doing. This also means that if we know the other won't be in for a particular evening one of us is not waiting around for a romantic evening.

What's more we can also plot in our days off throughout the year ahead, and make the most of our time with each other. A day off is sacrosanct so nothing or no one intrudes without mutual agreement.

is for Mortgage

EVERY COUPLE NEEDS somewhere to live. Finding a place of your own must be a priority especially when the wedding day looms nearer and nearer!

There are two obvious choices: (a) to buy; (b) to rent.

Some couples do not manage to find accommodation of their own and end up living with one or other set of parents. This situation is not one to be encouraged as it can present a whole host of problems and pressures. Part of marriage is leaving your parents' home and setting up home together in a new household. It is important to establish your own identity as a couple. If you live with parents you may still be seen very much as children. Obviously house buying can be a very stop-and-start business and you may need somewhere to live for just a week or two. We would still encourage you to make this as short a time as possible.

So how do you go about buying a house? Most of us are not in the position to buy a property outright so we need to arrange a mortgage. We remember when we did this. All of a sudden we felt very grown up, It must have been the idea of borrowing all that money!

Taking out a mortgage

The first step. The first step in the mortgage maze is to find out how much money you can borrow. In order to do this it will be necessary to visit the building societies and banks in your area. Some will see you without an appointment but others prefer an arranged time. It is a good idea to dress fairly smartly and have the relevant facts, like your annual salaries, easily accessible (a monthly pay slip will do), so that you can answer any questions you may be asked.

When we tried to get our first mortgage we walked up the high street visiting all the building societies. It was very depressing when we were refused at every society. There was one more to try and we went in holding out very little hope. Amazingly enough we were offered enough money to enable us to go for the house we had seen. It is always worth trying all the possibilities.

These days most building societies will lend two and a half times the joint income. For example:

His salary	£10,000
Her salary	£ 7,500
Total	£17,500 x 2.5 = £43,750

This couple could expect to borrow £43,750 from the building society on a mortgage. It is not necessary to buy the most expensive house that you can afford. Remember that mortgages have to be paid every month!

The second step. You now know your price range. Now is the time to go house hunting. There are many estate agents who will be able to furnish you with house details. Know in your mind what type of property you would like, eg flat (purpose built or converted), house (terraced, semi-detached or detached). Decide upon the area(s) you would like to live in and go to the estate agents in the same area. Most agents make an appointment for you to view a house; some accompany you.

When viewing a property it is a good idea to take the details with you and to jot down anything which strikes you while wandering around. If you look at a lot of properties it is amazing how easily you forget what they are like. Interior decoration can be changed quite easily and comparatively cheaply. The important points to look for are: is the house laid out as you would like it; is there enough room and moreover do you like it?

When you have found a house you like and can afford, make an offer. Don't be afraid to return to the house again to view it for a second or third time. You will be spending a lot of money, after all! The offer should be made to the estate agent either in person or by phone.

The next step is up to the person selling the house (the vendor) to accept or decline the offer. If accepted it is all systems go. You need to instruct a solicitor to act for you. You do this by phone, by letter or in person. Your building society or bank can recommend a solicitor if you do not have contact with one.

The third step. You will need to provide 5% of the selling price of the house as a deposit. The rest of the money is usually provided by the building society as a mortgage. Approach the building society and ask for a firm mortgage offer. Remember, you may not need or want to borrow the maximum. The more you borrow, the higher the monthly repayments. Think very carefully before finally deciding.

Types of mortgage available

Repayment mortgage. The capital sum borrowed plus the interest are repaid, normally over twenty-five years, but the length of time can be flexible. You also pay for a

Mortgage Protection Policy which gives life insurance cover.

The advantage of this type of mortgage is that if you get into financial difficulty you can extend the term and therefore reduce the payments, or you can defer payment on the capital and pay the interest only for an agreed length of time.

The disadvantages of this type of mortgage are that you don't get full tax relief for the whole period of time and there is no savings element.

Endowment mortgage. You pay the interest only on the amount borrowed. At the same time you pay money into an endowment policy which accumulates over the period of the mortgage. At the end of the term there should be enough money to repay the initial amount borrowed with some money left over.

The advantages of this type of mortgage are that you get full tax relief for the whole period, the endowment policy is portable and can go with you each time you move, this method is designed to be a way of investing.

The disadvantages of this type of mortgage are that there is no guarantee the outstanding balance will be paid back, if you get into financial difficulty there is little you can do but convert to a repayment mortgage; when interest rates are high this can be more expensive.

Pension plan mortgage. If you have a Personal Pension Plan you can link it into a mortgage. It would be a mortgage where you paid interest only and instead of having an endowment policy the PPP is used. At the end of the term the proceeds from the PPP are used to pay off the outstanding balance on the mortgage and you can opt either for a cash lump sum or a pension at retirement age.

Extra costs.

* Buildings insurance—this is obligatory.
* Contents insurance—this is optional (see 'I is for Insurance').
* Payment protection plan against accident, sickness or unemployment. This is again optional.
* Valuation fee for building society survey—this is obligatory.
* Indemnity premium—one-off payment payable at completion.
* Solicitor's fees.
* Private survey—this is in addition to the building society or bank survey and is optional. Ensure that you get a figure quoted to you before issuing instructions to carry out the survey. It is usually quite expensive, but advisable, especially on an older property.
* Stamp duty

The fourth step. Once you have decided which type of mortgage to go for the building society or bank will, in due course, issue an offer of advance in writing. Then all you have to do is wait for the completion of searches and for the exchange of contract date.

Solicitors normally take a minimum of six weeks to execute the legal work and need to be regularly chased by you if you are in a hurry. The offer of advance normally takes about two weeks. The solicitor needs written confirmation of the advance before the completion can take place.

You will be given the key to your property by the estate agent upon completion. The house is then yours (and the building society's, of course)!

Renting

Many young couples start their married life renting their accommodation. There are agencies dealing solely with rented accommodation and some estate agencies have a department which deals with renting.

Once you know which area you would like to live in find the appropriate agencies and visit them. They will be able to let you know what is available and to arrange viewing. It is important to make sure that any agreement entered into is on a legal basis. Alternatively, you may choose to enter into a private renting agreement. Again, this must be done on a firm legal footing.

Decor

When you take possession of your new home it may not be decorated quite as you would like. It is important at this stage not to attempt to do too much at once. If you are near the wedding you do not want to exhaust yourself by decorating morning, noon and night.

As a couple you need to decide what colour schemes you would like to follow in which rooms. We took possession of our first home about ten weeks before our wedding. We wanted to do everything before we were married but soon realised that we couldn't. Therefore we decided to decorate our bedroom and spent a long time choosing wallpaper, paint and curtains. It was a large room and wasn't finished before the wedding day. However it didn't matter. Decorating together it was Mike who demonstrated the expertise. Once finished we loved it and it was very much our room.

In order to change the appearance of a room you do not need to spend much money. Lining paper and paint, with perhaps an attractive border, can make all the difference, as our current residence demonstrates. Old and somewhat tatty furniture can be transformed by throwing over brightly coloured blankets or sheets. Floor coverings can be very expensive but stripped and varnished floorboards are very attractive (and fashionable) with scatter rugs. Curtaining is expensive but charity shops, jumble sales and relations often supply excellent bargains.

If possible concentrate on colour which can give a unifying appearance to bits and pieces around the house. Whatever the decor it will always look better when everything is clean and sparkling, so make that your aim.

The bare necessities

Having acquired your house you will now need to start thinking about what you will require when you live there. Starting from scratch is very exciting but can also be expensive. It might be a good idea to add one or two ideas to your wedding list such as a box of basic groceries, first aid kit and cleaning materials.

We have listed some basic necessities in order to act as a rough guide and prompt to your own thinking. Please play around with this chart, adding or subtracting as you choose.

Tinned goods	Household goods	Dry goods	Groceries
Tomatoes	Matches	Tea	Vinegar
Baked beans	Tin foil	Coffee	Instant potato
Tuna	Greaseproof	Salt	Oxo cubes
Pie fillings	Paper towels	Pepper	Cereal
Fruit	Dish cloths	Flour	Mustard
Kidney beans	Scouring pads	Rice	Dessert mixes
Various veg	Washing liquid	Sugar	Marmalade
	Toilet rolls	Herbs	Jam
	Soap	Spices	Marmite
	Toothpaste	Cocoa	
	Candles	Spaghetti	
	Bin liners	Pulses	

N

is for Negotiation

UNDER 'P IS FOR PARTNERSHIP' we deal with the whole issue of communication. In this section however we wish to look at the ways in which at times we must negotiate with one another in order to take decisions with which we both agree.

Depending upon your strength of character, education and upbringing you will find it either easy or difficult to take decisions. It really doesn't matter where you find yourself here. Nevertheless, you will very quickly discover that life turns on decisions. While as a single person you could regret but get away with bad decisions, once you are married your decisions affect someone else.

Mike is a very decisive person. He has not always been so but as he has matured he has developed a capacity to decide something and go with it. There is one situation though in which he detests making decisions. That is when he is relaxing. As far as he is concerned, once he is not working he doesn't want to be decision-maker.

Katey on the other hand prefers someone else to take the lead. Partly this is because it was the role Mike adopted from early on in their married life and she didn't challenge it but rather went along with it and actually found that she quite liked it.

Difficulties arose when Mike would ask Katey what she fancied doing on a day off. He wanted her to be the decision-maker, but she replied that she didn't mind. This frustrated Mike and led to argument, atmosphere and the waste of a good chance for a relaxing day together. What could make it worse was if Mike took the initiative at that point and at some time during the day Katey made reference to the fact she'd rather be somewhere else. Guaranteed thermo-nuclear explosion from Mike!

In discussion together we aired the problem (in similar terms to those above) and came to some practical conclusions:

For Mike:

A bad decision was better than no decision at all.

He really wanted to organise something Katey wanted to do and not assume that what he initiated was OK.

He couldn't abdicate all responsibility for decision-making just because it was a day off.

For Katey:

Decision-making was as much Katey's responsibility as Mike's, and not just limited to days off or when Mike felt like sitting back.

She must communicate her preferences in order that Mike could see he was investing time in a way that pleased her.

Decisions had to enjoy the clear support of both Mike and Katey.

As a result some very healthy talking went on. In order to achieve what we had identified, a number of practical steps were introduced. For example on days off, or as one approached, Mike would list a number of options with a request that Katey either choose one or play a random card and go for something completely different of her own making. Alternatively, he would ask Katey to think through and organise the day off. This also meant that surprise was reintroduced into Mike's life since he would be entirely in Katey's hands.

This is an outline of what we understand by the term

negotiation. Much as some politician or diplomat there are occasions when we cannot assume our way is the right or only way. We must consider our partner and *create space for debate and discussion before reaching our decision.*

This subject of negotiation is particularly important in six key areas. We have set them out below:

1. Career/Vocation

At the start of your marriage you may both be working. You may be in the fortunate position of enjoying your job. Again, you may be pursuing a vocation such as nursing or teaching. This is fine until one of you is offered promotion which entails a geographical move. Is the promotion sufficient reason on its own to move? Is the partner who stands to lose their job through the move prepared for that?

When after three years of marriage Mike considered a request from his employers to move, he first took it to Katey. She was at the time teaching in a comprehensive school in the Midlands and doing very well. After discussion we decided to move with Mike's job which meant Katey resigning her teaching job.

The consequence was that she was unable to find another teaching job and had to teach supply which she finds most dissatisfying. So there was a cost for her. It was essential therefore that the decision had been discussed and agreed before any action had been taken.

Of course, not to accept promotion might mean either retrenchment or even redundancy. Sometimes such are the costs involved in maintaining a strong marriage. The number of divorces as a result of job relocations is appalling. If you cannot move in agreement either wait till you can or stay put.

What if the children are grown up and the wife is considering a return to work? Traditional thinking that the wife's place is in the home may need to be challenged. Also, many women returning to work face a crisis of confidence and husbands will need to be attentive, sensitive and supportive.

Finally, if one of you is made redundant or is unemployed there is a need to be sensitive to the stress of that situation. Often the unemployed partner can feel they are not contributing effectively to the household and are in fact the weak link in the relationship. The 'working' partner, if we can put it like that, needs to be practical and caring in the way he or she involves the unemployed partner in the daily decision making and invests them with dignity.

2. Relocation

We have looked at moving house in the light of promotion or a change at work. However, there is great importance in involving your partner in all aspects of moving house. We heard of a couple where the husband went ahead with buying and selling the family home without telling his wife. You can imagine her shock when she suddenly learned her home was sold and that she was moving to a property she had never seen!

Often more is invested in the bricks and mortar than pounds and pence. Individuals develop a sense of security in where they live and in their neighbours round about. Therefore it is important that you come to a common mind when considering moving.

3. Finance

It is important that each partner in the marriage is free to spend the 'loot'. In 'D is for Daily Budgeting' a lot of this ground is covered. This is a reminder that all major purchases should be discussed together and agreement reached on the item in question, and the price band in which to spend.

Mike has an interest in ornithology and regularly looks at catalogues of birdfeeders as he seeks to attract a wider diversity of birds to the garden. However, he will always talk it through with Katey before he makes an order. Likewise, Katey will check with Mike the budget she has on going to the sales or out to look for a new outfit. In fact Mike often goes along as well as he enjoys picking clothes for Katey.

4. Leisure

Again this is covered in its own section yet we need to be sensitive to each other. A couple we know well are affected at this level. The husband is a keen and devoted carp fisherman. This entails sitting at the lakeside night and day, the worse the weather the better, in the hope of hooking a large fish. Once landed, weighed and photographed the fish is returned to the water. Well, it takes all sorts! In order to follow that interest they sit down and plan the fishing trips into the diary ahead of the season. Time is negotiated and set in place. Each knows the score and life goes on untroubled.

It is essential that our partner at no time feels they are being replaced by a hobby. Agreement is essential therefore over time allocations to our leisure pursuits. We must turn the tide on computer widows/widowers and ensure our hobbies refresh us and enrich our marriage.

5. Role

Entering marriage we may carry a load of unhelpful assumptions concerning our expectations of our partner; for example, she will cook my meals and wash my socks; he will plumb in my washing machine and decorate my house. The problem may be that neither of you have the skills nor inclination to meet your partner's expectations.

The idea is that in marriage you should complement each other. To do that you first have to establish what each other is gifted in. Then identify what each other is interested in exploring.

When we first married Mike never cooked. But over

the years he has developed both an interest and a skill in that area. Katey meanwhile has taken to exploring gardening. Often, once the mystique is removed it is easy to apply ourselves to something we have never tried before. We know of couples where she is the best decorator and odd job person; he is best deployed cooking and child minding. We must talk these things through and not assume. We must not criticise our partner on the basis that they are not fulfilling what we assumed they would, and we must become creative at inventing alternative lifestyle patterns.

6. Preferences

Both partners in any relationship will have preferences with regard to how they envisage the marriage developing. There will be aspirations as to what they see their partner becoming in the years ahead. These can act as a trap. You must own your aspirations for your partner and yourself as these will subtly affect your thinking and influence your decisions.

One of the most difficult problems in any marriage when there is an unresolved dispute is to avoid getting locked up to each other. When each of you is convinced that, finding a *modus vivendi* is virtually impossible.

We are always struck by the fact that of the many couples who come to us because their marriage is apparently failing, the first contact is made only when the situation is well out of hand. It's like the fire brigade being summoned to a burning building, but on arrival discovering that the fire has such a hold they cannot extinguish the blaze.

In preparing couples for marriage we always advise them to seek out a couple known to and trusted by them both, who have several quality years of marriage under their belts. We encourage them to develop this friendship so that at moments of stress they can go and get advice and assistance. So often the bleakest of situations lightens once shared with reliable friends.

There are certain ground rules to be observed. Never talk about an issue outside of the marriage without your partner knowing that you are going to do so. You do not require their permission but it is important that you do not act in an underhand way. Often the very fact that you mention speaking of the issue outside the privacy of the marital home is sufficient to provoke the situation to an amicable resolution.

Also, never confide exclusively in a member of the opposite sex. The hackneyed phrase 'You see, my wife doesn't really understand me' has been the beginning of more extra-marital affairs than one cares to mention. The objective of calling upon the wisdom of others is to strengthen your marriage; not to solicit sympathy or recruit supporters.

With the loss of the extended family in our society and the common practice of children marrying and moving some distance away from their parents the informal network of advice has all but disappeared. Therefore we must recognise that we cannot survive on our own, nor are we intended to. We can learn a lot from others, and relationships with other couples can provide a wealth of helpful hints through to advice which will help our marriage at difficult points.

We have appreciated the advice and support of trusted friends at times of difficulty or pressure, such as the time we had to contend with the thought of remaining a childless couple. Therefore seek out such friends and do not be afraid to call upon their help. If you do find that you have no one to whom you can turn then contact the organisation Relate. Their address and phone number are in the phone book under Relate. However, you may need to wait several weeks before an appointment.

O

is for Offspring

CHILDREN ARE STILL assumed to be very much a consequence of a successful marriage. Ever since on their creation God instructed Adam and Eve to 'be fruitful and multiply' in the opening chapter of the Bible, this has happened with almost monotonous regularity! However, children do present us with some important questions. There are significant repercussions to what can appear a relatively simple decision to have children. They can prove to be an impossible strain upon the relationship as easily as they can prove a source of delight.

At this point pause to complete the following questions. Each of you should complete it independently by placing ticks in the appropriate column. At the end of these questions further direction will be given.

	Very much	A lot	OK	Not a lot	Dislike
I want kids.					
I enjoy kids					

I enjoyed
my child-
hood

I like my
parents

I liked
school

You should both have a completed table of ticks. They will provide you with ample material for talking together as an entry point into the whole subject of children.

It cannot be assumed that everyone both likes and enjoys children. Sometimes one partner can express a strong affection for kids which the other partner feels it impossible to do anything but assent to. Then several years into marriage the issue of going for a baby causes both tension and disagreement, simply because the subject has never been discussed.

We have had young marrieds with a couple of years' marriage under their belt come to us and with a certain amount of nervousness enquire if they are wrong because they do not feel they want to have a family. Our response is to check carefully the reasons, but if they have properly thought and talked the issue through we have no difficulty with a conscious decision not to start a family. Such decisions are not final and can and should be reviewed from time to time. Many such couples have devoted the time which would have been invested in children to community service, either within the UK or overseas.

Sometimes, however, our experiences of childhood can themselves deeply affect our view of parenting; both our desire to become a parent and our sense of ability to carry such responsibility. If we have had difficult childhood experiences we should communicate them to our partner. He/she is marrying into our history as much as our present and the consequences of past experiences have a significant impact on the marriage we will build.

Therefore, in the light of the above chart, talk through parents, school days and childhood experiences and memories. If there are real bleak spots which are a source of emotional pain you may be advised to get some professional help from a counsellor. This could be organised through an informal conversation with your GP or your local church leader. Alternatively, a conversation together with a trusted and mature friend can release a lot of the emotions which have been bottled up for years.

We have known someone who was totally unable to bring herself to talk about her childhood years. She never recalled stories from the home she had grown up in and gave no indication of having any affection for her parents. It was as though there was a whole portion of her life over which a curtain had been drawn. As a result she was determined to avoid creating the same climate for her own children yet, having never talked the issues through, she was totally dependent on her wisdom alone in handling their upbringing.

The difficulty became acute in her children's teenage years when a serious break occurred, similar it turned out to the one which she had experienced herself. It took many years of hard work to recover the relationship between her and her children. Perhaps some of the pain could have been avoided through frank talking at an earlier stage. The family home could have been better prepared and the couple better equipped for parenting. Talking together and learning from each other can help us all to avoid repeating the mistakes we felt we were subject to.

As we pointed out in the section on engagement, our childhood and teenage experiences can severely shape our perceptions and determine our ability or otherwise to handle relationships. Our partner must know who they are marrying, and the question of children often brings anxieties to the surface.

Once you have established your personal view on children you may need to engage in discussions as to how your personal and different perceptions can be brought together. Do not bring children into a divided household. They will pick up and eventually play on the differences between you. Even where you take a radically different view on some action taken by your partner (eg a disciplinary issue), wait until you are alone before discussing it. *Do not disagree in front of the children.*

Starting a family

Agreement over the timing of this is essential. The trend is to leave starting a family later and later. This enables both partners to pursue a successful working life before babies arrive. With modern methods of contraception available, control over the timing and number of children is in most instances in the hands of the couple themselves.

This has obvious benefits, yet there are hidden difficulties. When for example children are delayed until the quality of life desired has been established by the couple, the children ultimately may be expected to 'fit in' to the dream lifestyle existing within the imagination of the couple. Unfortunately babies seldom do. They will play havoc with your SPALA (Stripped Pine And Laura Ashley)* home. The quiet evenings disappear and life begins to be dictated to a necessary degree by the routine of the child.

You both need to be honest about how selfish you are. Are you available to serve one another by each fulfilling

---

*We are indebted to Phil and Julie Stokes for this helpful descriptive item.

turns with the baby. Are you creating space for this infant to express itself in your home or more concerned about maintaining a sense of sterile cleanliness throughout ensuring your house reflects the centre spread of *Homes & Gardens* rather than a family residence? Toys and a measure of untidy chaos will enter your home together with that new babe.

You will need to reorder your lifestyle. Perhaps both of you have worked up to this point. Now the child will prevent this; it requires attention and care twenty-four hours a day. The following must be given some thought. Will you:

1. Take a traditional line and allow the wife and mother to continue at home to invest in bringing up the baby?
2. Act radically and explore role reversal with the husband and dad leaving work to look after the baby?
3. Follow the increasing trend to each follow your careers and employ a nanny to take responsibility for the child?
4. Involve immediate family members (grandparents, for example) to provide support in the child's upbringing?

These issues should be well discussed in the early years of marriage. Many men retain a very traditional view of family and are threatened by the thought of working mothers. This can prove aggravating to women who feel totally frustrated by childrearing. It may well have a bearing on geographical relocation should that mean moving away from close family.

Obviously there are laws concerning maternity leave for which the wife will continue to receive a measure of income. Some enlightened companies are also offering paternity leave these days!

Each of the above approaches is workable but which best suits your personality, objectives and budget?

Preparing for a family

Once you have decided to try for a family then preparations need to be made. Is there sufficient space in your accommodation? If you are not planning to have a 'family bed' it is helpful for the child to have a room of its own. This retains your own distinct relationship as a married couple and creates a sense of space and territory for the baby.

There is no need to invest in all the sentimental nonsense that is all part of the baby industry today. You will obviously want to make the nursery special, but this is far more for your satisfaction and enjoyment than for your offspring's since they won't notice if the walls are white woodchip or Peter Rabbit! However, some form of visual stimulation is recommended for the baby's benefit.

It is essential to draw up a budget for the baby's arrival or you may be surprised by the costs. We have drawn up a list of essential items below. Take a trip to your local supermarket and discount chemists and price the items so that you begin to see the real costs of preparing for Baby.

The Jayne Scott basic baby list

Baby
6 babygrows for use day and night (cheaper on packets of three)
4 bodysuits (vests) (cheaper in packs of two)
3 cardigans
2 pairs of mittens
1 bonnet (2 if a winter baby)
1 pramsuit if winter
1 sun hat if summer
1 shawl

Changing
changing bag

changing mat

Nappies

(a) Terry nappies

24 terry nappies
4 pairs of waterproof pants
200 disposable nappy liners
nappy pins
nappy bucket with lid
1 kilo sanitising powder

(b) Disposable nappies

(These vary in price and size. A newborn gets through
between 5-8 a day. They are cheaper when bought in bulk.)
nappy sacks

Bath

2 hooded towels
1 baby bath

Toiletries

top and tail bowel
zinc and castor oil
cotton wool balls
cottonbuds
baby wipes
baby talc
baby soap
baby shampoo

Feeding

(a) Breast

2-3 good fitting nursing bras
nipple cream
disposable nursing pads

(b) Bottle

6 bottles (cheaper in packs)
spare teats
cold water steriliser (alternative steam steriliser)
bottle brush

sterilisation tablets
6 bibs

Miscellaneous
baby nest
brush and comb set
baby chair/bouncer

Finally, be assured Baby's arrival will also affect your current lifestyle. One of you will need to stay in of an evening to care for Baby. You are therefore not as mobile as you were; especially as a couple. Of course over the first few months Baby can travel with you and it is worth while borrowing or buying second hand a travel cot for this purpose. Once a little older your wings will be clipped unless you have a long line of willing babysitters.

Also, you will be on night duty, and interrupted nights of sleep lead to tiredness and irritability. Most mothers we have spoken to speak of feeling desperate for sleep at times, and support for them from sensitive husbands is essential. This is when family members living close are invaluable.

There will also be the need to guarantee space away from Baby in order to retain sanity. Plan carefully to get out together and keep enjoying your relationship. Also, keep up your social friendships. If Mum (or Dad) is with Baby all day she (or he) will need adult stimulation at regular intervals.

Childlessness

Of course there is the possibility that you may discover that you are apparently unable to have children. The likelihood is one that slowly dawns as you keep trying to conceive but don't.

If you have been trying to start a family for a year without success it is worth while making contact with your GP. Initially, he or she is likely to have a friendly conversation with you and ask several questions about your sex life with your partner. It is helpful if you can attend the surgery together for mutual support, but beware many men feel highly threatened by the thought of not being able to father children.

The initial test will normally be a sperm count to check the viability and motility of the man's sperm. This involves masturbating into a glass jar and can be done at home or at the surgery or hospital if you have been referred to an infertility clinic at that stage. The only important factor is to get the glass jar to the laboratory (all organised by GP or hospital) before the sperm dies.

If the sperm passes, then a referral to the infertility clinic will enable further investigations to discover why conception is proving a problem. This may involve surgery. If there is little that can be done surgically there is today the possibility of 'test tube' babies. There are moral and financial implications to a decision to proceed in this direction, and you and your partner will have to talk seriously about such matters.

The overriding impact of infertility, especially for the woman, is the emotional consequences. This can lead to irrational and extreme behaviour and requires great support, strength and understanding from the husband. It is a circumstance which will test individual character and the commitment of the couple to their relationship. It is essential not to keep silent but to find sensitive and trustworthy friends in front of whom you can be yourselves and who can provide a measure of external support.

If you do face infertility, and just because you have one child it does not mean you won't face secondary infertility, then there is an organisation you should contact for information and advice. This is: National Association for the Childless, 318 Summer Lane, Birmingham B19 3RL. There is also a helpful book detailing our own experiences in this area entitled *Two's Company*.

Testament of Childlessness published by Kingsway Publications or available from the EA, Whitefield House, 186 Kennington Park Road, London SE11 4BT. You may also choose to explore the possibility of adoption or fostering, and again the infertility clinic should be able to provide you with information to begin that process.

Along with childlessness there is the possibility that you may give birth to a handicapped child. Everyone carries a level of anxiety on this issue, especially during pregnancy. It is essential that as a couple you have talked about your attitude and approach to such a situation should it occur. Own your fears and anxieties. These are not intrinsically evil. Again, each situation cannot be faced in reality unless it occurs, but to have aired your thoughts and fears is helpful. Should you produce a handicapped child there are specialist societies and self-help groups, details of which will be available through your GP, Citizens Advice Bureau or local library.

If the principles of honest communication are retained then all further issues such as the children's education can be worked through effectively.

We have not dealt with divorce, and children from a previous marriage at this point, as it is dealt with specifically in 'U is for Unfaithfulness'.

P

is for
Partnership

MARRIAGE INTENSIFIES THE boy/girl relationship. Together under one roof wedlock enables your relationship to become more intimate, more continuous and more demanding. We discover things about each other that we had never even slightly suspected before. The way he sits on the bed and picks his toes; her litter of dirty laundry decorating every surface of the bedroom. These are the issues that bring tension and argument.

It sounds obvious but in marriage we must learn to accept each other for who we are. Mike remembers an earlier relationship with a girlfriend where he thought she had all the potential to be shaped up to become a most suitable companion for him. However, he learned the hard way that people are not lumps of modelling clay to be shaped by the master potter. Rather they are individuals with a past and a history of experiences which have formed their personality and character. To treat someone as a thing to be modelled to meet our personal requirements is an abuse of their humanity and must be avoided at all costs.

The whole purpose of marriage is not to manipulate and control our partner. We are called to be liberators, not dictators. This involves the challenge of creating space for each other and allowing individuals to be who they really are. Yet a number of us have very little idea of our partner's character and personality in detail. We simply know that we have met someone whose company we enjoy and with whom we have fallen in love.

Below, you will find several questions which we would like each of you to answer honestly and then discuss your answers together.

1. Family Background:
(a) What elements from my family home do I want to bring into my marriage?
(b) What elements do I want to leave out?
(c) What is my happiest childhood memory from home?
(d) What is my unhappiest childhood memory from home?

2. Social Adjustment:
(a) On a scale of 1-10 (10 being excellent) how do I rate my ability to relate socially?
(b) How do I react to other people?
(c) Do I talk positively or negatively about people I've met socially?

3. Intellectual Development:
(a) Am I more or less intelligent than my partner?
(b) How many books do I read in a year?
(c) Do people with qualifications threaten me?

4. Vocational Development:
(a) What is my work?
(b) Am I happy in it?
(c) What I would really like to do is . . . . (fill in the blank).
(d) Do I see myself pursuing a career?
(e) What am I prepared to sacrifice for my career?

5. *Leisure Interests:*
(a) How do I use leisure time?
(b) My favourite hobbies are . . . . (make a list).

6. *Spiritual Development:*
(a) Am I more or less spiritual than my partner?
(b) The type of spirituality I enjoy most is . . . .
    (fill in the blank).
(c) What are my gifts?
(d) What is my spiritual objective?

7. *Sexual Experience:*
(a) How have previous sexual experiences affected me?
(b) Are there areas I should communicate to my partner?
(c) Am I relaxed or tense with regard to sex?
(d) Am I worried about anything related to sex?

8. *Physical & Mental Health:*
(a) Have I suffered from any serious physical or mental
    illness?
(b) On a scale of 1-10 (10 being excellent) how would I rate
    my health?
(c) Do I find the thought of any particular illness difficult
    to contend with?

When we marry we need to remember our partner's history as well. All of us have been shaped by our experiences; psychologically, emotionally and spiritually. These experiences leave their mark and may trigger certain reactions to a given set of circumstances. This can be most disconcerting for our partner. Therefore it is essential that we understand as much about each other's past as possible.

Marriage is a relationship; indeed a lifetime's relationship. Hence it is most important we take seriously the relational experiences we have each had. These more than anything else can cause friction within the present relationship we are seeking to build.

While we are all *products* of our history, we need not

be *prisoners* of our history. Through owning the areas where we have been scarred growing up, we can find ways forward together which will lead to great personal fulfilment for each partner, and a cracking good marriage relationship.

A marriage relationship should afford sufficient security to enable each partner to drop their defence mechanisms and feel entirely safe. This should be your aim.

Conflict

Conflict is an inevitability of any relationship. Marriage is no exception. The nonsense propounded by the film *Love Story* that 'love is never having to say you're sorry' has to be ignored. Love is very much about the willingness to say, 'I am sorry,' and to mean it. This is the true stuff of romantic love and is essential to establishing an effective relationship together within marriage.

The problem with conflict is that we often feel guilty or ashamed of the fact that there is conflict within our marriage. Sometimes we pretend everything is wonderful when we have spent the whole of the previous night in tears. Relationships will inevitably produce wounds. Wounds lead to resentment. This in turn generates hostility and this hostility can precipitate a war. The problem with all wars is that they lead to fatalities and our society is fast becoming littered with the debris of broken marriages.

The answer is to avoid the war. This is easily said, but how do we do it?

One story which highlights the humorous side of these situations was related to us by the wife of a couple with whom we were staying. In the early years of their marriage she had become irate with the way her husband came home from work, picked up the newspaper and ignored her. She therefore decided to ignore him entirely. After several days, during which time he had apparently failed to notice that he was being ignored, she gave up on this approach feeling even more rejected than when she'd started! Instead she decided to raise the issue and they were able to talk it through constructively. He hadn't considered she might feel ignored. He was simply doing what he'd always done and needed a dose of progressive education!

Again, several days before our first wedding anniversary, Mike, was telling a joke to a couple of friends as we stood around drinking coffee in the kitchen. Katey made the unfortunate mistake of interrupting to give the punchline. Mike saw red, reacted and threw boiling hot coffee over Katey. She left in tears, the couple diplomatically excused themselves and Mike had to decide whether to stand his ground or follow his wife upstairs, eat humble pie and apologise, seeking to explain why he had overreacted to such an extent.

Fortunately he followed the latter course of action and sought to put things right. A wrong decision at that point could have led to a major problem. The ensuing conversation helped Mike to explain his sense of anger at being upstaged and Katey's embarrassment that here was a joke that had been regularly trotted out by Mike and no doubt everyone had heard. Reconciliation was achieved and an area of the relationship that needed working on identified.

Interestingly we were censured by another couple who heard about the incident. The friends who had witnessed the whole thing and had made such a tactful withdrawal were engaged to each other. We were told that our behaviour in front of them would not have helped them get a proper view of marriage. They are now successfully married and have been for a number of years. We believe they got an honest insight into the realities of wedded life which did them no harm.

Throughout marriage we need to learn to recognise the verbal and non-verbal messages our partner is sending. Mike knows from the tone of voice when called to table if he can afford to finish what he's doing or needs to attend forthwith. Again at a party he can recognise instantly what is being said to him across the room by the look in Katey's eyes. We do well to learn to pay attention to such signals. In so doing we can avert conflict most effectively.

At all times conflict arises out of choices. On all occasions we are responsible for the choices we make. This is helpful. The cries of: 'It's all her fault'; 'He's totally unbearable!' and the like seek to lay blame totally at someone else's door. This is a somewhat selfish and naive approach. Two people involved in a relationship must accept mutual responsibility for the situations they find themselves in.

Hence we can choose if we are going to allow the conflict to develop or nip it in the bud. Each of us can take personal responsibility for the scale and nature of conflict within our marriages. After all, it's not conflict but rather the ability to recognise and resolve it that matters in the end.

Each of you should make a commitment to the other that you are more interested in resolving conflicts than furthering them. Whether they involve the replacement of the toothpaste cap or changing jobs, discuss how you will find ways of approaching the other and airing your grievance, justified or not, in the interests of maintaining an honest relationship.

For many years it has been recognised that sharing life in depth with another person is the solution to most of our human problems. It is in loving and in being loved that we find real meaning in life. However, seeking such closeness which is in itself an answer generates conflict. The consequent disillusionment can make or break the relationship. This is why active communication is so important.

At this point it would be good to do a brief exercise together.

1. Together, identify those incidents and factors which generate conflict within your relationship.
2. Identify, in as far as you can, the sequences which generate such conflict, eg mood, tone of voice, behaviour pattern, etc.

Affirming each other

Many of us have grown up under constant disapproval. From parents, teachers, employers and friends we have developed a strong picture of our weaknesses and what we can't do rather than our strengths. We in our turn find it easier to criticise than to affirm people. Most of our conversations over lunch or out for a drink involve pulling people apart rather than speaking warmly about them.

The tragedy is, many of us are as much victims as perpetrators of this. When we come to marriage we hear all too clearly the negative comments and fail to pick up the word of encouragement. All of us in our marriages need to take a definite decision to compliment and build up our partner. This affirmation generates trust within them for us, creates a greater measure of security within the marriage and helps us to begin to think rightly about ourselves. We take on board more of what people say about us than we can imagine, so let us not add to the load that has been built up over the years.

When Mike was growing up he well remembers it was generally joked, 'Don't let Mike carry the plates; he'll drop the lot!' The concept that he was clumsy stuck with him over the years and he would refuse to undertake certain tasks because he was clumsy. One of these was a reticence to hold very young babies. Now, while this is somewhat lighthearted, it well illustrates the point about the importance of what is said to us.

However, this is not a licence to go around saying all sorts of positive things for the sake of it. We need to be realistic and address obvious weaknesses as well, in case we should become resentful at what appears to us our partner's apparent non-performance in certain areas.

As a start, try the following exercise together. You will each need a piece of paper and a pen. Write your answers down privately and read the instructions before sharing together.

1. List three strengths you recognise in your partner.
2. List three weaknesses you recognise in your partner.

Instructions for sharing.
Strengths: Guys should share the strengths they have identified about their partner first; then girls should follow suit and share with their fellow.
Weaknesses: Girls go first this time and fellows follow on.

The reason for this order of communication to each other is to underline the point that men are so often slow in encouraging and affirming their wives. It is good to take time to communicate those qualities you appreciate; to notice special additions around the house.

When it comes to weaknesses men are the worst at receiving criticism, however kindly it is meant. Wives know their husbands best and if the men can hear what their wives see as weaknesses, which everybody else has probably noted anyway but is too inhibited to tell them, then husbands can be creatively shaped to become more whole human beings.

This process is one that should be regularly repeated throughout marriage as it provides a good basis for healthy communication.

Finding ways to communicate

1. Interrupt the sequence leading to conflict. This may take courage, but get into the habit of doing it. We struggled over the way Mike picked his nose and the way Katey ate an apple. Mike would suddenly get a

sharp rap across his picking hand and as Katey nibbled away endlessly Mike could feel his blood boiling. We therefore learned to acknowledge our weaknesses and request we were given a warning or expressed our frustration early and without any edge.

2. We must exercise trust and confidence in each other. Mike is no TV lover. He prefers reading but cannot concentrate when the TV is on. However, if he asked whether the TV needed to be on, or left the room to read elsewhere, Katey felt he was making a statement about her watching TV and what she was watching. Therefore Mike mentions he is leaving to read or enquires if Katey is using the TV for anything more than moving wallpaper, while indicating verbally that he has neither a problem with her watching or the programme.

3. We must learn to apologise and take responsibility for our bad behaviour. In the early years of marriage Mike would often storm out of the room and disappear off out of the house. When he returned there was no word of explanation. Katey was left with an awareness that she had upset Mike, but didn't know whether or not she was culpable. Learning to say sorry and to acknowledge to your partner that you are out of order is essential.

4. We must work through the possibility of rejection and the increased hostility such rejection can produce. There are times when an apology has been thrown back by one of us in the other's face; there are occasions when the process of defusing a situation has been hijacked by the refusal to co-operate on the part of the other. This is the learning curve we need to ascend. Remember, there is no gain without pain and it is the truly tough who get going when the going gets tough!

5. Learn to decode each other's verbal and non-verbal messages. Tones of voice and knowing looks can

aggravate or educate; probably they do both. Wisdom leans towards treating such indicators as educational tools in order to prevent the deterioration of the situation into all out war. The passage of time allied to experience is the great secret here. Mike recently returned home from church much later than Katey, who was feeling unwell and had opted to go to bed early and catch up on her sleep, had expected. The tone that greeted him as he came through the door immediately alerted him to the fact that he was walking into an ambush: one false move, or word, and he would be dead. He therefore kept it lighthearted, refused the bait, went out of his way to be helpful and survived. Several days later he challenged Katey who acknowledged she had felt aggrieved and fancied a fight. Apologies made, another lesson learned and no casualties!

6. We must always remember that we are building a relationship and serving our partner over and above ourselves. Many have made the mistake of winning the argument but losing the person. We cannot afford to behave in this way.

7. We must recognise the true nature of stress in order to deal with it effectively. The question is: 'Do we have stress or does stress have us?' It is our perception of people and issues which finally counts. That is what causes us to act in certain ways. Mike still can't walk into a school building without his stomach knotting up. His childhood perceptions persist to this day. Practical advice and help from our partner will not go amiss here. They may not know all the intricacies of the situation, but they do know us and they can help reflect back to us on an issue from outside the situation.

Learn these communication skills together and enrich your relationship.

is for
Questions

WE HAVE GATHERED together some of the most pressing questions that may occur and given a brief way forward to help you on your way to finding an answer. There will be things that cause us anxiety during our marriage. To sit and stew over these generally does little to help us. If we do not feel talking it through with our partner has eased the problem then we should look outside the marriage for help. But always with our partner's knowledge.

Obviously our partner may not want us to talk to anyone apart from themselves. However, not to do so courts disaster for the very relationship itself. Often, to have a helpful perspective from a neutral reference point can help put things into perspective. We stress *neutral* because it is all too easy to get support from a close friend who totally accepts our position and gangs up with us against our partner.

Someone who is neutral can help you as a couple by reflecting back what is going on between you both; things you cannot see because you are too close to the situation. One of the saddest experiences is talking with individuals whose marriages have failed but who with the benefit of separation and distance from their spouse can see all the half-truths they accepted without challenge and how they were manoeuvred by the one they loved. A neutral sounding board would have helped the couple to recognise this while there was still time to do something about it, or revealed that one partner (or both) did not have the will to work at repairing and renewing their marriage.

What is marriage?

This is an essential question. Our answer will in many ways determine the extent of our commitment to making our marriage work and succeed. Our view is that the central meaning of marriage is covered in the text of the Christian marriage service. If this is the way we have chosen to begin our marriage together it is not inappropriate to understand a little of the thinking and convictions which lie behind the words we will be using.

In the first book of the Bible you will discover God creating mankind in His own image. 'So God created man in his own image, in the image of God he created him; male and female he created them' (Gen 1:27). Hence both the man and the woman are God's image bearers. They were also created for each other (Gen 2:21–23), and the words associated so closely with marriage are also found in the early chapters of Genesis: 'For this reason a man will leave his father and mother and be united to his wife, and they will become one flesh' (Gen 2:24).

These words apply to both members of the partnership; not just the male. In other words, at your marriage there is intended to be a leaving of the parental home and all it represents. You as an individual break from the protection and provision of your parents—always assuming this was something you had known which is not a foregone conclusion by any means today—and commit yourselves to provide provision and protection for each other.

Not to sever the links with the childhood realm in this way is disastrous. It leaves the door open to either side's parent(s) having an unhelpful level of access into your relationship. It also means you have not totally committed yourself to your partner and have left room for a retreat back into your childhood home as and when convenient.

The intended process is *to leave* the influence of parents while entering a new relationship with them as a couple. You are *to cleave* or commit yourselves so closely together that nothing can be driven in between you to act as a wedge and force you apart. This includes work, friends and leisure activities. You are also *to become one flesh*; to begin a sexual relationship together which is exclusive to you and your partner in marriage. However, the 'one flesh' principle extends beyond the realm of sex to include an equality of opportunity and leadership within marriage. (See 'X is for Xantippe' and 'P is for Partnership'.)

If we were to continue with our look at the Bible we would also discover that the concept of marriage, that is 'leaving, cleaving and becoming one flesh', preceded mankind's estrangement from God. Therefore it is God's intention for men and women to work out their relationship together within the context of marriage.

The church has often been accused of having a negative attitude towards sex and sexuality. On the contrary, God invented it and always intended that sexual union should be fully enjoyed but within the context of an exclusive and committed relationship. It was not limited to marriage because mankind's corrupt nature meant that a containment strategy had to be developed to deal with his sexual appetite. Rather marriage predates man's fall into sinfulness in the biblical record. We should therefore accord both marriage and our sexuality a high view. Mankind was designed for a lifelong monogamous relationship with a member of the opposite sex.

The Bible goes further. It also lays out clear parameters

within which marriage can be worked out successfully. Many of us think we know best or that we can work things out for ourselves. Unfortunately, given the high divorce rate and the loss of Christian faith within our society, to hold such a position is increasingly untenable. Not many of us would consider repairing a car engine without a trusty Haynes manual. The Bible is just such a manual for life in general and marriage in particular.

Always remember that marriage is not simply a piece of paper, ie the marriage certificate, nor simply a rather grand ceremony. It is a relationship intended for life which requires hard work and commitment within a clear framework. We believe that the Bible gives the best framework within which to establish a successful and enjoyable marriage.

Where do I get help?

We hope this won't be a regular cry of anguish within your marriage. However, you may meet a period when for various reasons what you had has gone a little sour; you are not apparently getting on as well together; some issue has arisen which is causing you some grief.

Elsewhere we have mentioned how to handle marital conflicts in detail ('N is for Negotiation' and 'P is for Partnership'). Broadly speaking, there are three routes:

1. Consult a trusted and unbiased friend. There is a lot of accumulated wisdom in people, but we don't have many contexts in which we can draw upon it. Do not consult someone who is strongly biased towards your opinions or who is not committed to seeing your relationship succeed. For some, a parent can play this role and traditionally that is where you would have gone for help. However, be careful that you are not giving an unhelpful lever which could threaten your relationship long term.

2. *Make contact with the local church leadership.* Most have a fund of experience in matters concerned with relationships and spend a good proportion of their time giving practical counsel to married couples. This is a further informal way to get assistance.

3. *Contact Relate.* If you want a more professional approach then contact Relate. Details can be found in your telephone directory, from your local Citizens Advice Bureau or from your GP. The only difficulty is that you may have to wait for an appointment. All counsellors have been trained for the work of marriage guidance and will probably want to work with you both over a period of time.

There is no shame in seeking advice as a married couple. Neither is it a sign of weakness. However, neither of you should engage in seeking significant counsel without your partner's knowledge. The pressure of the situation may demand that you do it without your partner's consent, however.

We would say you ought to talk with someone if you feel that you have made a mistake in marrying the person you have, find difficulties with sex, or your partner begins to hit you. Misplaced loyalty which suggests that to seek help is to betray your partner is a nonsense. Relationships reveal different strengths and weaknesses in us all and we may need advice on how to turn a weakness into a strength.

Finally, the people you speak with as suggested above will not think any the less of you because of your situation. They are prepared to listen and counsel primarily because they are committed to marriage, and successful marriage at that.

Cross-cultural marriage

With a shrinking world more people are marrying someone from a completely different culture from the one in
which they grew up. This offers some special oppor-
tunities (some might say difficulties but we are opti-
mists) in working out a marriage relationship.

If you meet your partner overseas and decide to get
married be aware that you will have to contact the Home
Office in the UK to check out their status and right of
entry to the UK. This should create no problems, but we
have talked with folk for whom this has meant some
work before everything was ready to roll.

You would also be advised to learn as much as you can
about your intended's culture. Read about it; look at an
atlas; find communities of their culture and background
within the UK.

There are special issues raised by cross-cultural marriages, not least in learning to understand each other and
how most appropriately to communicate. Your British
culture might mean you are fairly clear in saying what
you feel. Your partner may come from a culture where
you don't express things directly but only by inference.
These are the areas of learning that lie before you both.
Take your time and get help from those within the same
culture as your betrothed.

Also, don't assume your partner is either familiar or
comfortable with the way of life in the UK. Everything
needs adjusting to from visiting a GP to running the
bank account.

Financial difficulties

Consult chapters 'F is for Finance' and 'D is for Daily
Budgeting'.

Miscellaneous

Adoption. You will need to make contact with adoption agencies. Many will write back with pro forma letters saying they are not looking for parents at present. This can prove very disheartening but will test your resolve to adopt. Eventually you will be accepted, then a long series of interviews will be the order of the day while you are both assessed as to suitability. If eventually you are successful you will need to wait until a baby/child is available and the society thinks it is a suitable match to you and your partner. Stamina is most definitely required.

Adopting from overseas is still frowned on by social services in the UK. If you intend to go down this route then you will have to be prepared to deal with a lot of red tape, and to defeat every bureaucratic barrier that is raised, and many will be, to obstruct you. If you decide upon a cross-cultural adoption you must discover all you can about the child's cultural roots so that as he grows up you can help him discover something of his national identity.

Of course, if you are in a position to adopt a child with a handicap then you are likely to be welcomed with open arms.

Fostering. Contact your local social services and they will advise you of the way forward. Details are to be found in the telephone book.

Bereavement. Contact your local GP for advice and referral for more specialist counselling. It is not unusual to go through quite a period of mixed emotions. Sometimes there are physical ramifications as well. This is a period during which your partner will need to be exceptionally sensitive and patient. It is also a time when expressing what you feel, from anger to despair, is essential, and your marriage is a safe environment in which to do this.

131

is for
Relocation

THERE ARE VERY FEW people who move into their first home, raise their children in it, become grand-parents while living there, enter retirement and end their days still in the same house. Society is very mobile these days so we can expect to move house every so often. Your type of employment has a direct bearing on this.

When we first married, Katey was teaching full time and Mike was employed by British Youth for Christ. Mike's job involved a move every eighteen months fow a while and so we became experts at relocating. There are many issues involved. We had to decide whether we were both happy with the pattern we were establishing. For example, it made it quite difficult for Katey to keep changing jobs and she didn't always manage to secure a new post. We talked this through and Katey decided that she was quite prepared to resign from teaching in order to follow Mike's job around the country. When things got tough, it was important that Katey had to come to the conclusion on her own and was not just toeing the line put forward by Mike.

So you have to move. How do you go about it? The first decisions you have to make concern area, housing and how to afford it. The section 'M is for Mortgage' goes through house buying with a mortgage in detail. Once you know where you are moving to, if you have a property to sell this should be well underway. It is vital to co-ordinate buying and selling so that you (a) don't end up living on the streets or (b) end up with two mortgages to pay—even for a few days this can be very expensive. The solicitor doing the legal work should be able to work towards simultaneous exchange of contracts.

When everything appears to be set up and going smoothly you must consider the actual move. There are a few more decisions to make. Are you going to move yourselves or are you going to employ professionals? We have moved ourselves once and used a removal company every other time! From that I think you can guess our prefence.

Moving yourself can work very successfully. It is often done because it appears to be very much cheaper. You need to look very carefully at all the costs to work it out:

Hire of van
Petrol
Lunch for helpers
Tea, coffee, etc
Breakages

We also think that 'wear and tear' on the personnel involved should be added as a legitimate cost.

Professional moving costs tend to be a one-off payment which covers moving costs and insurance. You need to add the cost of refreshment breaks.

We have tended to move nationally rather than locally which also adds a time factor which your helpers should consider.

So, if you are to move yourselves you need to book a van in good time. If you are having a removal company you need to contact them three to four weeks before your projected moving date. It is good to get at least three estimates so that you can compare prices and the service they offer. In order to arrange for an estimate ring the removal companies. They will ask for your projected date and destination and arrange for an estimator to call. This person has a quick look around your house, and makes notes on what is to be moved. It is important to tell him what is and isn't going to be moved. Don't forget the contents of the shed, the garage and the loft.

Removal companies also offer other services such as packing china and breakables, packing books or even packing everything! Obviously these services have to be paid for, but you may find that you want to use some or all of them. Removal companies provide packing cases or tea chests.

When you have decided on which company to use, book it! Removal companies are accustomed to dates changing, but you must keep them informed. Some companies offer a 'free removal package' with every estimate. Katey always gets one of those estimates because she likes playing with key bags and sticky lables!

As moving day looms you have to get organised. Now is the time to sort through all your possessions. There is a rule in our house that if it hasn't been worn or used for a year it's out!

If you are moving yourselves, or at least doing all your own packing, you have to decide when to start. Some people have the space to pack and put all the packing cases into a spare room. Other houses do not afford this luxury so it seems like you are living 'in limbo' for weeks. We have always tried to pack up in just two days. It is two days of chaos, but we find that preferable to four weeks of semi-chaos.

The most nerve-wracking part of moving is packing breakables. The answer is plenty of newspaper! Do not skimp on this because it is the cushioning of the newspaper which can stop breakages. Do not pack boxes or cases too full.

What about books? Our house has always been full of books. We both did history degrees and have books to cover most historical periods. Our first mistake was to fill large boxes to the top with books. Even Tarzan would have struggled to lift those boxes! We always like to label each box with its general contents and to which room in the new house we would like the box to go. If, for example, your new kitchen is too small to accomodate all the boxes, direct them to another room nearby.

One point is to remember is that some removal companies like to take their packing cases away with them so they will have to be emptied on arrival. We also find large bin liners invaluable for packing lighter, softer things as cushions, towels and linen.

Make sure that the last items packed, and therefore the first to be unpacked, are the kettle, mugs, coffee, tea, milk and sugar. (Removal men need to keep their sugar level up—it's hard work!)

Removal men take full responsibility for packing the van. We remember one removal man who wanted to saw our sofa in half to fit it in the van (it was a joke—we think). If you are doing it yourself, take advice on how best to pack the van with all your worldy goods.

So, those are the mechanics of moving. There are, however, other jobs to do. When leaving one house it is important to inform all the people who supply any services. This means th at you will eventually receive at your new home final accounts which need to be settled. The following authorities need to be informed:

Gas
Electricity
Water
Telephone
Community charge

Also inform:

> Banks/building societies
> Credit card companies
> Storecards
> Library
> DVLC

You will be visited by officials the morning you move to take the final meter readings. They are quite used to the chaos in which you will no doubt find yourselves.

It's important to inform friends and relations of your new address. Most removal firms can supply you with change of address cards. Otherwise you can buy them or design your own. Our last move was a week before Christmas so we enclosed our new address with the Christmas cards!

Moving is not an easy pastime. Katey finds the whole event very traumatic whereas Mike embarks upon it as a new project which needs creative solutions.

The end of moving day needs very careful planning. It is not the time to invite friends and relations to see your new home. You need to have a good meal (courtesy of friends or the local take-away), ensure the bed is made up and have an early night. Tomorrow you can start to play house.

*is for
Sex*

THIS OF COURSE may seem the most obvious of the subjects to be covered in this book. After all, sex is as easy as falling off a log! Unfortunately, this is not what every couple discovers.

We have counselled couples who have enjoyed an active sex life with various partners before their marriage but have struggled to sustain any sexual activity within the relationship. Others have never got off the starting blocks, and yet others have established a pattern whereby the man is happy having an orgasm but gives no thought either to giving his wife pleasure or avoiding causing her pain. It is not perhaps quite so simple.

If you have any questions about the mechanics, ie where everything fits, then get advice. Either get a graphic book on the subject or talk together with your GP. It amazes us that in an apparently so liberated society as far as sex is concerned, we are so reticent to talk about it in any other terms apart from real or imagined conquests. There is no shame in acknowledging that you are a novice as far as sex is concerned, and we recommend that you enter marriage with your virginity intact. It was intended to be preserved for the marriage relationship and society would be the better for an outbreak of sexual morality.

Once the mechanics are clear talk about what you intend for your first night away after the wedding. We give guidelines for this in 'H is for Honeymoon'. However, as far as sex is concerned be aware that you will have had an exhausting day. The thought of sex may be not the most delightful, especially in comparison to a good night's sleep. There is no failure in this. It is plain realism. If you are tired, sleep. Ending the wedding day with sexual intercourse is not a prerequisite for a successful marriage.

Plan the first night together beforehand. Express any embarrassment you may feel at the thought of peeling off your clothes in front of your partner or having your partner remove them for you.

It is also a good idea to take a honeymoon support package. You may find a tube of 'KY' jelly or equivalent proves useful in providing lubrication for sexual union. This can be applied to the penis and the vagina as part of the foreplay. It is also good to be aware that if the sheath is not being used you will discover a wet patch appear in your bed after sex as seminal fluid runs back out of the vagina. In the interests of equality, make him lie in the wet patch from time to time! Tissues are also therefore helpful.

Never rush at sex. Learn to appreciate your own and your partner's sexuality. This will require exploration of each other's bodies; discovering what pleases. This also means talking to each other and explaining verbally what is good and what is not quite so good. Learn to communicate freely during your foreplay. It took Mike a while to adjust to the fact that Katey would often crack a joke at what appeared to him to be an inopportune moment. In fact it took Mike a couple of years to learn how to relax fully into sex. But it was time well spent and an important lesson!

Sex itself is intended as a developing experience. It is quipped from time to time that if you were to put ten pence in a jar every time you made love in the first year of your marriage you would spend the rest of your married life emptying the jar. There is a measure of truth in this. Sex is meant to be a journey of exploration together. If it is simply about 'getting one's end away' then the whole act has been robbed of its purpose in securing and deepening the marriage relationship.

As one lays down good wine, likewise sex is intended to improve with age. We have gone through periods when we have neglected our sex life. This is very easy to do and very quickly it falls into disrepair. We are both so often shattered at the end of the day that the thought of lovemaking then is not that exciting. Therefore we have to plan mornings and other parts of the day carefully so as to find the right time for sex.

It does not matter who initiates sex. Gone are the days when the male initiated and the female lay back, closed her eyes and thought of England! Both partners should initiate. It is very disconcerting if the male is always expected to initiate. He can begin to feel that his wife doesn't really love him because she is making no advances towards him. Hence the importance of mutual responsibility in this area of initiation.

Again, it does not need to be left to bedtime. A suggestion that sex would be fun can be communicated early in the evening, and the evening can slowly lead in that direction. Alternatively, surprise each other by organising a romantic meal. Creativity and fun are the order of the day.

Throughout our marriage each of us is to be experience not performance orientated. The idea is to give pleasure to each other. Seeking to emulate some film star stud is not the best way forward. It's not making the earth move but your partner happy that counts in the end. Therefore don't be afraid to express what pleases you and keeps you interested in sex.

We have learned from an excellent book written by John and Christine Noble called *Hide and Sex* a most important phrase when it comes to sex. It is simply this: 'As long as you break no bones everything is permissable.' Obviously your partner needs to be in full agreement, and you both need to be supple enough to explore various positions. In the book *Hide and Sex* and the manual *A Touch of Love* by John Houghton, a number of intricate positions are detailed for your amusement and enjoyment.

A word here however on fantasy. It is unhelpful to become controlled by your fantasies. Your partner should provide sufficient stimulation for you. If they do not you are likely to have problems. So be clear to whom you are making love. For this reason we are not in favour of dressing up or bondage sex since it begins to move you away from the reality of deepening a relationship with your partner and entering a realm of unreality.

Problems

With regard to problems that may occur, time is usually the way to discover the answers. The man may find a problem with premature ejaculation. This will settle down once you develop your experience in sex. It is very common in the early stages of marriage, but as the man becomes more skilled he will be able to control the moment of orgasm and indeed should so that he ejaculates as and when his wife is happy. Often simply slowing the pace down and taking your time helps on this issue.

Female orgasm is another area of concern. We recognise that all women can achieve orgasm but that it is not essential to successful lovemaking. Again, exploration will enable you to discover together how to attain this. Don't be surprised if it doesn't happen overnight.

Also men can experience periods of impotence when they cannot sustain an erection. This is often related to times of stress. Do not be alarmed; it will pass. If you are concerned then have a chat with your GP.

You may discover that you find it impossible to penetrate with your penis. In this case persevere using fingers to help gently stretch the vagina. Also use KY jelly as a lubricant. If you still fail to couple successfully both pay a visit to your GP for some advice and help.

Finally, what if you decide you don't like sex and don't want sex? We would advise that you visit your GP to explain the situation and seek referral to a sex counsellor. Often our attitudes to sex have been set in place through upbringing and experience, hence we may need to unlearn some attitudes before we can proceed. Obviously it is not healthy to decide to exclude sex from the marriage.

It is also worth noting that some women go off sex altogether after having a baby so you will need to talk extensively at such a time and together determine how best to go forward.

Conclusion

It is worth remembering that when we get married we give our bodies away to our partners. They are not ours any longer. Therefore we cannot use sex as a means of control over our partner. The Bible, where we have turned to before for advice, points out that neither the husband nor the wife can withhold themselves from each other. So don't use sex as a means of reward. This is an abuse of your partner.

t

is for
Troublespots

WHEN WE GET MARRIED we have to remember that we are marrying each other's backgrounds, upbringing and past experiences. We are each an amalgam of what's happened to us, how we've been treated and our opinions. This means that there are more than likely to be areas of conflict because of different understandings and perceptions. These need to be confronted head on before they develop into full-blown 'no go' areas. We have pinpointed a few such areas which may well emerge!

In-laws

There are many 'music hall' type jokes about in-laws which are, to say the least, unhelpful. When you marry, your relationship with your parents enters a new phase. You are no longer a child, therefore the ground rules for a successful relationship need to change. Upon marriage, of course, you also enter into relationship with your partner's parents on a new level. These relationships need to be handled carefully but clearly from both sides if success is to be achieved.

Clarity in a situation and in relationship helps to keep

things on a good footing. It is well worth communicating clearly so that everyone knows where they stand. Prevarication on an issue will often lead to a very tangled web. By being clear you are being fair to yourselves, your parents and your parents-in-law. Clarity also suggests forthrightness. It is impossible to be clear and yet not put your opinion or position in a forthright way.

Having said this, it is important not to be aggressive for the sake of being aggressive. It is possible to present a point of view and have a discussion in a mature adult way. It is through such discussions that all concerned can come to an understanding of a positive relationship. It takes time and energy but it is well worth it.

To reach a relationship of this type it is tempting, on occasion, to give in in order to keep the peace. You are bound not to agree on everything immediately, but do not be tempted just to give in. You will not always be right but neither will your parents. This relationship is one where no one should rule anyone else. Parents should not rule children but children should not rule parents either. Parents and children should seek to set each other free within the newly-formed relationship. It is lovely to see parent-child relationships having developed into really good solid friendships!

On occasion you may feel that there is a conflict of loyalty between your partner and your parents. It is important to remember that your first loyalty must always be to your partner and therefore he or she should be put first.

A discussion point which often arises in a marriage, later rather than sooner, is what will happen to my/our parents when they get older? It is impossible to tell any couple what they should do because each situation is so very different.

There are various options which it would be good to discuss with your parents if that is possible. Do they want to relocate, and if so where to? They may want to live near one of their children but much consideration has to be given to moving. It means leaving friends and neighbours who have, perhaps, been a part of their lives for a long time. Familiarity can be a great comfort and this is also true of surroundings, so have the people concerned considered the major change such a move will involve?

If a move to a remote or coastal area is considered, have they thought about what life will be like in such a community in the winter? It may have been a lovely holiday spot, but day-to-day living tends to be different.

How will they react if the relation they have moved to be near then moves? The motivation for moving must be clear and not dependent on other people's actions.

One possible scenario which must be considered is how would one parent cope if the other died and one person was therefore left alone?

There are no right or wrong answers to these questions, but they need to be discussed and considered, in advance if possible.

The situation of having parents to live in your house with you may well arise. It really should be discussed openly and honestly with all concerned. It might well involve other brothers and sisters who will obviously be concerned about their parents. Before having parents to live with you do consider these points:

1. Is your house big enough to sustain a good relationship together?
2. Will you be able to accept each other's lifestyles?
3. What financial arrangements have you made?
4. What arrangements have you made with regard to domestic matters?
5. As a family (you, your children, your brothers and sisters), are you happy with the situation?
6. Are your parents happy with the situation?

Stress/illness

Living life at the end of the twentieth century means that we are often subject to stress. Stress is defined in *The Shorter Oxford English Dictionary* as 'force or pressure'. Stress is a common complaint these days so it is as well to have considered how to avoid it and also how to deal with it.

We had been married for three years and were living in Milton Keynes. Mike began to experience inordinate tiredness and lethargy. We put it down to early mornings, late nights and lots of hard work in between! As the weeks passed there was no improvement; in fact Mike appeared to have even less energy. Eventually a visit to the doctor was arranged. We were shocked by the diagnosis and also the treatment. The doctor suggested that Mike was suffering from an unknown virus and that he needed complete rest. Well, complete rest for a human dynamo like Mike is not a very welcome suggestion. This situation, unfortunately, lasted for about six months. During this time Mike was not 'ill' in the classic sense of the word, but he needed looking after and encouraging a lot of the time. One Christian visited him and as his parting shot told Mike to 'pull himself together' and get back to work! Not a very helpful suggestion. Days seemed very long with no pattern to them. He would walk to the paper shop, buy a paper and sleep off this major exertion. Thankfully, the test matches were on TV so Mike could wile away the long days playing armchair cricket.

Katey had a lot of adjusting to do during this period. Having been used to a husband who was always in control and taking a lead she now had to take over as the number one decision-maker. Both of us found this a difficult situation which naturally created its own level of stress. Dealing with this stress was valuable experience, although at the time we didn't quite see it that way! Some of the lessons we learned were:

1. Be honest about how you are feeling, to yourself and your partner.
2. Don't be afraid to take time out by yourself.
3. Make sure you have someone to whom you can talk freely and honestly about the situation you find yourself or yourselves in. This is not failure, it is sensible use of friends.
4. Find an activity you find to be a real stress reliever—walking, running, cycling, listening to music.

After six months Mike eventually received prayer. This finally sorted the situation out and Mike returned to work. It had been a valuable time—we'd walked, talked, picked blackberries, shared our frustrations and learned a little about stress!

Christmas

You may think it odd to have included Christmas in the troublespots section. This is because such an important celebration can often be the cause of so much argument. One of the reasons for this is that we each have our own expectations for the festive season, usually derived from our childhood experiences.

Our first Christmas together we decided to spend alone in our own home. We told both sets of parents in good time so they knew what was happening. We also made arrangements to see them soon after Christmas for family celebrations, but we wanted to be together, just the two of us, on December 25th.

This was where the fun began! We both had set ideas on how Christmas should be celebrated and proceeded to plan, each of us on our own, what would happen. We bought a seven foot Christmas tree and trundled back with it through the streets of Wolverhampton. We had bought a few decorations and some lights for it and proceeded to dress the tree. As a child Katey had not often been allowed to decorate the tree as she was the youngest of three and had to fight to make her presence felt, but now that she could decorate at her leisure the thrill had gone!

The next 'problem' was when and where we should open our presents. We discovered that we each had different expectations for this great event. What we should eat and when we should eat it was a problem to be discussed and what we should do with all the time Christmas Day affords. Looking back we realise how important it is to talk such issues through and then to begin to establish new traditions of your own.

Mansion/detached/semi/terraced/flat/bedsit

Where you will live as a newly-married couple needs a lot of consideration. There are lots of factors to take into consideration:

1. Geographical area
2. Type of home
3. Money available

Getting a mortgage and renting are dealt with under 'M is for Mortgage' but you still need to decide on the type of home you would like. Many people automatically choose a similar home to that of their parents, but does it really suit your lifestyle? A large family house may be necessary when children come along but a flat can be easier to keep clean and tidy for two; especially when they are out working all day. It is also cheaper to run, which may prove significant.

The choice of living accommodation must be a joint decision so that husband and wife will both feel that they had a say in where they set up home together.

The size of the accommodation must also be determined by the volume of possessions needing to be housed. Also, are you intending to have visitors to stay regularly? Will you be entertaining folk at meals? These questions should all have a bearing on your choice of property.

We started out married life in a four bedroom, detached house in Wolverhampton. It was a bargain due to its location. Five weeks after our wedding three people moved in to share our home with us! Obviously we couldn't have lived like that in a one bedroom flat! Decide on your accommodation/lifestyle priorities and then select the type of housing that will enable you to fulfil those aspirations at a price you can afford.

Decorating your new home is one way of setting your stamp upon it. Finance again enters the equation but imagination can cut a good number of corners. One word of caution: don't strip the walls from top to bottom of the house in one go unless you know you can complete the job of redecorating immediately. Living in undecorated accommodation for a long period of time can prove most dispiriting. We once lived for four months with wallpaper stripped from the kitchen (an everyday room), so we know. Remember, a little and often is a most acceptable route forward. Unless you're intending to move on in six months.

With the redecoration you can find creative ways to express your personality in the house. Make sure you are in agreement about the final decisions and that each of you makes a contribution.

The place to start with decorating is to choose the colour scheme. The actual decorating can lead to all sorts of fun and games. Katey brought no decorating experience to marriage, while Mike with his little knowledge cast himself in the role of expert and perfectionist. The first room we decorated was the bedroom. Mike allowed Katey to paint the skirting boards—a backbreaking job which few visitors comment upon—with two undercoats and two topcoats. She was closely supervised throughout! Mike hung the paper, with Katey's assistance of course, and during which time he shouted at her not a few times. He also did the rest of the painting. However, as time went on Mike mellowed and Katey spoke out and she was entrusted with more difficult tasks to execute and through which she could express herself and make her own contribution. We learned how important it is to give each other room to develop and practise new skills.

Diet

Before marriage you may have been living in your family home, on your own or with mates. Wherever it was a pattern of eating was established with likes and dislikes, together with favourite dishes. Now you are to share both mealtime and food. Your partner's food fancies may not coincide with yours; you're a red meat devotee, he's a vegetarian. Accommodation of each other needs to be made. When presented with something which has made you heave since infancy, please be tactful; never compare the platter of food you receive unfavourably with what you were used to in the parental home.

It is important to eat a healthy diet. It is reckoned most men accumulate the weight they later seek to lose, often under medical instruction, within the first two years of marriage. This is through contentment. It is worth taking steps to avoid this if you can.

We are not of the school that sees the wife's role as including shopping, cooking and washing up. If both partners are working it is even more ridiculous to think roles can be established in such a way. Turn shopping and cooking into a corporate activity if you want some fun. Alternatively, indicate which of you is taking responsibility for which areas, and swap around regularly to save getting into a humdrum rut. Indeed, troublespots should provide an effective challenge to keep you from becoming boring and settled. So be encouraged.

U

is for Unfaithfulness

PERHAPS THIS IS something of a negative section to include in a book which is looking forward to and encouraging us into marriage. However, it is clear that many people enter marriage with a measure of fear for the future. Indeed every one of us should be realistic. Unfortunately, when we get married our interest in the opposite sex does not disappear or become wholly absorbed in our partner. If this is a shock to either of you then you had better start talking earnestly.

Today in England nearly two out of every three marriages are ending in divorce. This has serious consequences; first for the couple who have observed their relationship come apart before their eyes. There are large areas of emotional hurt to work through; bitterness to be confronted and dealt with; often an overwhelming sense of guilt to contend with.

We have stood close to a collapsing marriage on more than one occasion. The pain is intense and the road to healing is often long and arduous.

Secondly, if there are any children they too are deeply affected by the divorce. They have lost the stability of having two parents under the same roof. They will lack either a male or a female model. They will also be unable to observe how marriage works and so have no role model to guide them when they approach an adult relationship with someone of the opposite sex.

Apart from the chaos this introduces to society at large it leaves deep psychological and emotional scars on us all. It is therefore because of increasing incidence, likely contact with marriage failure at some point in our history and in the interests of being able to take steps to prevent it that we have included this section on unfaithfulness.

Obviously it is essential to be honest about any fears we may have with regard to our partner's potential marital unfaithfulness. Raising the issue should not threaten the relationship nor be interpreted as an accusation by one or the other. If we fail to acknowledge our fear we will discover we are watching our husband or wife with eyes like a hawk and seeking to circumscribe their activities. We will find it hard to believe they are really going out for a drink, or to visit a friend. Everything in us will try to probe and in every way but directly indicate we don't trust them. Since all relationships grow out of the soil of trust we begin to destabilise our marriage without even realising it.

Jealousy is an emotion which we all need to guard against. It is neither healthy nor helpful. It leads our imagination in all sorts of directions; none of which enhances our respect or love for our partner. There is nothing worse than returning home with a spring in your step and looking forward to seeing your partner, only to be met by a string of questioning that makes the gestapo appear moderate in approach. Immediately, tension is introduced and what should have been a good evening together relaxing is lost.

The only way to avoid jealousy is to keep an open account between yourselves. If you have suspicions, mention them. If you are attracted to someone else, be honest about it. Once something is aired it has far less ability to harm us. However, do be thoughtful about how and when you communicate. The style can determine the reaction. So learn to be wise.

In our early years of marriage Mike travelled extensively with his job. This meant he was away from home for several days at a time. While away he would be meeting people and naturally found some of the women very attractive. However, the ground rule laid down by us was that Mike would phone home every day and talk to Katey. This actually meant organising his time and locating a phone. Also on returning home Mike would tell Katey what he had been doing and also say if he had felt tempted at any level. This was helpful and nonthreatening to Katey and strengthened the relationship.

One other lesson we learned early in marriage is the potential harm words can do. The old adage 'Sticks and stones can break my bones, but words can never hurt me' is totally false. Words go deep into us and wound. What's more we can begin to believe what is said and live under its shadow becoming an embodiment of someone else's opinion about us. Do not at any time privately or especially publicly, pull your partner apart verbally. No matter what the provocation, save it until you are on your own and sort it out then.

A programme of monitoring and accountability like this, established with the agreement of the couple, is an excellent safeguard for marriage. Talk through how you will act as a safeguard for each other in this area.

In the church where we are involved we each have friends to whom we can also be accountable in areas of weakness. Hence we have an extra safeguard for our marriage and a framework within which to talk through any areas of weakness within our moral character.

At all times the watchword for avoiding marital unfaithfulness is 'opportunity'. If we ensure that we are *avoiding every opportunity*, ie being alone in the office with that attractive young lady from personnel or allowing ourselves to be driven home by that handsome hunk of a manager, then we are building practical safeguards against anything untoward.

A final word on this is that boredom often leads to opportunity. If we fail to pay attention to our partner and create quality time together with them then problems can emerge. For example, if our work absorbs a large proportion of both our time and our energy, and we find we are leaving home early, returning late and always exhausted, then it is little wonder that our partner begins to lose interest in the relationship we have promised to build together. No relationship can be adequately sustained by one member. Should someone begin to flatter or spend time with the one who feels deserted or rejected in favour of work, do not be surprised if an extra-marital affair is born.

This is why it is so essential that we take time to relax together and discover activities that we enjoy doing as a couple. Look up 'L is for Leisure' for more on this particular subject.

Background

A word or two here about background. It may well be that you are a product of what is called a broken home. Your own parents failed to make marriage work and you were brought up by a solo parent. Obviously the timing of your parents' separation is important as to the effect it will have had upon you. Regardless of that, however, you will carry a greater anxiety about marriage failure than others. It is tragic how breakdown and divorce increasingly runs in families.

Having observed a marriage breakdown you have also been prevented from seeing a marriage worked out or modelled before your eyes. You will have seen the parents of your friends, but they were no doubt on their best behaviour when you were around. You will have heard about the rows they really have from your same friends.

But you won't have seen anger dispersed and dispute resolved. This is something of a handicap.

Therefore you must be clear about your aspirations for the marriage and the ideas you have formed about how it all works. If the reality does not live up to the imagined ideal then you have a problem.

Alternatively, you personally may have experienced a marriage breakdown. As you prepare to enter marriage again all sorts of spectres may have to be faced. You will need to have talked through in detail the causes of the previous failure. Also, it is essential that the emotional hurts have had time to heal and that bitterness and resentment have been laid aside. We are convinced that bitterness and resentment can produce severe physical symptoms if they are not dealt with properly.

You will also need to talk through with your partner your fears and anxieties as you are on the verge of re-entering marriage. These fears may be quite irrational but if they are real then you must address them. You will also need to confront areas where bad memories are resurrected, for example the whole sexual relationship may need to be thought about carefully.

If you will be bringing children with you into the new marriage then they too must find time and ways of bonding with your new partner. The relationship should be between all members of the new family.

Reconciliation

What happens if you discover your partner has been unfaithful?

First, you need to establish if they are prepared to be honest about it. If you have had your suspicions and discover that there is an adulterous relationship taking place, you need to establish if your partner will acknowledge it. You then need to establish if this adultery will end or if your marriage will be sacrificed. It is at this time that wise, external counsel can be helpful since you will both be boiling over with emotions of various sorts.

Alternatively, your partner may have come to you and confessed their misdemeanour. Obviously this is slightly better since they are seeking to put the marriage back together.

To recover from such a betrayal of trust, which is what adultery comes down to, takes a big heart and a lot of courage. However, it *can* be done and many can testify to a successful marriage retrieved from the dust of unfaithfulness.

What is required is an honest apology and an offer of forgiveness. There is no way that such unfaithfulness can either be justified or ignored. What's needed is a breaking off of the extra-marital relationship and a clear, unequivocal apology. The boot is then firmly on the foot of the injured party. Will they find it within themselves to forgive?

Now forgiveness cannot be conditional. All sorts of thoughts flow through your mind but you can only forgive and forget. Obviously for the relationship then to develop effectively new ground rules will need to be established. These are rather like a cane that is used to support a plant that has been knocked over, in order to enable it to grow again. It is unable to support its own weight immediately.

If forgiveness is extended then full reconciliation can be achieved. It will take time to recover trust in each other. There will be painful conversations together and probably tears as well. But slowly the marriage will recover and have every opportunity to flourish again. However, the idea is never to get into this situation. Prevention is always better than cure!

V

is for Values

GATHER ANY GROUP of people together and raise a controversial subject such as capital punishment and you very quickly discover everyone has an opinion. Some opinions are strongly held; others less so. At times these opinions have been carefully thought through and are well argued; alternatively they are merely a cocktail of various threads of ideas accumulated over time and regurgitated with passion.

These opinions provide each of us with what is called our worldview. This very basically is our assessment of how things ought to be in the world in which we live; what we think is just and unjust; what we think is right and wrong. It affects our view of society in general and also our own personal morality, eg if there's no ticket collector at the station I won't pay my fare.

Our worldview provides the foundations upon which we build our life. It's illustrated by the following story: 'A wise man built his house upon the rock. The rain came down, the streams rose, and the winds blew and beat against that house; yet it did not fall, because it had its foundation upon the rock. But a foolish man built his house on sand. The rain came down, the streams rose,

and the winds blew and beat against that house, and it
fell with a great crash.'

Such simple wisdom highlights how important it is
that we build upon something substantial. There is no
sadder sight than a demolished house. In such a state it
cannot fulfil the purpose for which it was intended and is
of no real value. It reflects what it might have been but in
reality is no more than a pile of rubble.

It is therefore important that we think carefully about
the worldview we will adopt, and recognise that opinions can change. New information can mean we see
things in a different light; experience can redefine the
parameters of our beliefs. At all times it is important to
engage in constructive discussion with a wide range of
people as this helps us to appreciate their worldview and
to apply our perspectives to what we hear from them. It
also provides an opportunity to communicate what we
believe and why.

During your courtship you and your partner may well
have discovered that you have violently divergent views
on certain subjects. Hopefully you do disagree in some
areas or else the whole relationship will be very mono-
chrome in a technicolour world. Divergent views enable
us to discover creative forums for debate. Always remember we have two ears but only one mouth; try to listen
twice as hard as you try to enforce your viewpoint.

When we were going out together we found ourselves
radically disagreeing on a whole host of issues, many of
them moral. We would talk late into the night, neither of
us prepared to give ground. It was part of the learning
experience for Mike that he could learn from Katey; he
didn't need to win every argument.

Having majored in history at school and then univer-
sity Mike's view of debate was to win. Katey often
expressed the fact that if necessary he would argue white
was black; and win! However, winning an argument is

not necessarily the most creative approach to issues of fundamental belief.

On the other hand Katey had to discover a greater confidence in her opinions and to stick to her guns when arguing. She was always far more teachable than Mike and not at all fussed about winning arguments.

Through discussing such differences of opinion together you will discover to what extent you are threatened by someone else challenging your views. You will also learn how to engage in healthy dialogue over points of disagreement; again an essential marriage skill.

Below you will find an extensive questionnaire asking for your views on various issues. Go through and answer the questions independently of each other before joining together to discuss your answers with each other.

QUESTIONNAIRE

Belief

1. Do you believe in God?
2. Describe the God you believe in.
3. How do you know this God is real?
4. Are there others who share the same confidence in the same God?
5. Does this God take an interest in people in the world today?
6. How, and in what ways?
7. Do you communicate with this God?
8. How, and in what ways?
9. As far as you know does your partner share your faith in this God?
10. If so how do you express the reality of this shared faith together?

Morality

1. How do you decide if something is right or wrong?
2. On what basis would you be prepared to do something you knew to be wrong?
3. If your view is challenged, to what do you refer to support your view?

4. Is there, in your opinion, a final authority in all issues of morality? What is it?
5. What are the three most important moral issues that concern you today?
   (a)
   (b)
   (c)
6. Is your morality influenced by your belief or your belief by your morality?
7. Are there situations in your life where you have taken a decision or acted in a way which is against your moral code?

In discussing your answers together explore the question of the basis on which you made your answers to the questionnaire. Remember to listen to your partner's perspective; don't seek to correct them from your point of view. You are learning about each other.

Today we are increasingly confronted by a society which has adopted a morality of means to establish its values. It can be summarised with the phrase: 'If it feels good, do it.' The major problem with such a viewpoint is that it is primarily selfish. I see myself as the centre of the universe and so long as I am happy with my decisions then I will proceed. This individualism which pays only lip service to the fact that we live in a communal society is the seed of society's eventual destruction. With a shrinking world, the so-called global village, we must take a responsible position and realise that we are in fact our our brother's keeper and our decisions have an impact upon others' lives. We must therefore take others into consideration when we make both our public and private decisions. Indeed, our private world is directly related to the public and will determine how valuable a member of society we will be.

Where does worldview come from?

Parents: We owe more than we might care to admit to the values of our parents. We observe them more than any other individual in the earliest and most impressionable years of our lives. Mike can still vividly remember his father discovering he had been given too much money when cashing a cheque at the local bank and returning to give it back to the cashier.

The way our parents react to and handle situations makes a deep impression upon us and may well shape the way we react in similar circumstances as we pass through adolescence into adulthood.

It may also surprise you to discover that the majority of people adopt the political persuasion of their parents. So again, the deep influence of our parents is evident.

Reflect on the values that were paramount in the home of your childhood and identify the good from the bad; the ones you would want to emulate and those you would want to avoid. Also consider your own opinions and actions, and decide on those you are comfortable with and those you either want to change or subject to close scrutiny, uncertain whether you are keen on them or not.

Media: TV, newspapers and magazines all help form our opinions. It is a standing joke that you can tell someone's political leanings by the newspaper they read. Working in schools it is all too evident to what extent lightweight news programmes on the TV present young people with a set of opinions on contemporary moral issues which they immediately adopt.

It is inevitable that with the amount of television people watch their views are being set by what they observe. It's not just the news programmes. Soaps such as *Neighbours* also give a set of values by which a fictitious set of folk work out everyday life; resolving conflict, falling in love and building relationships.

We can be convinced that what we see on our TV screens is total truth. We can aspire to live as the fictitious characters we watch live; or be convinced that a certain viewpoint is the *only* viewpoint because of the way a programme is made. The media have an increasing role in giving us our opinions without us having to think about them.

Friends: Obviously we take very seriously what our friends think. Mike remembers vividly how hurtful it was when one of his friends dropped him once he discovered Mike had decided to become a Christian.

Especially in our teenage years friends' opinions matter and we talk more openly and honestly than at perhaps any other period in our lives. What our friends think of us is important. Among our friends we will find those who emerge as the opinion setters of the group. We disagree at our peril. Yet we must always be sure that we agree with what we are doing or participating in—even if such participation is passive.

Have you talked through to what extent your opinions are your own or just your friends'?

Observation and experience: We also pick up our value system in this way, often without realising it. This brings to mind the experience of a friend. Queuing with his son for some event, a couple pushed in front. This triggered the boy's sense of justice and he suggested to his father that they should force their way in further up still. However, his father addressed some significant and wise words to his son. He expressed his view that he did not want to have his behaviour dictated by the behaviour of others; that is, he was more than capable of forming his own opinions and determining how he would live— even if it meant standing at the back of queues.

All the above illustrate how important it is to set our own value system. We have found personal fulfilment through the Christian faith. The teachings of Jesus, which we quoted earlier in the chapter, provide a sure foundation for both private and public morality. We have also discovered a firm foundation on which to build every element of our individual and married life, and heartily commend it to all readers. We would be happy to send some literature on becoming a Christian to anyone who chose to write to the publisher requesting it.

We can also put ourselves under great pressure in forming and having confidence in our worldview. If we are either particularly insecure or ambitious we are likely to mould our values to suit our insecurities or ambitions.

Learning to know what we think and why we think it helps us with our insecurities. Then we have something to contribute to discussions with friends and can participate in setting the values in place for our marriage.

Ambition also needs to be recognised and rightly handled. Many folk have betrayed their values in the interests of personal ambition. This materialistic worldview must be both resisted and challenged. Each of you can maintain a healthy watching brief on each other to ensure that ambition does not take over.

It is important to have a clear and mutually agreed worldview as a couple. This will set the framework for your marriage in general and specifically when it comes to taking decisions with regard to work, education and use of holidays.

is for
Wedding

THE WEDDING DAY is the big event everyone works towards, and there is much to be done before the day arrives, so that it runs smoothly and legally! Depending on where you marry, and in what tradition, not all of the following will apply to your situation, but you will find the information you need to make the day run smoothly.

Church ceremony

In the Church of England there are four ways in which a marriage can officially take place. These are:
1. By Banns
2. By Common Licence
3. By Special Licence
4. By certificate issued by a Superintendent Registrar

1. Banns. These must be read on three successive Sundays in the parish church of each partner's parish. Application is made to the vicar of the church where the couple wish to marry. He will require certificates certifying that the banns have been published.

If no objection is raised, the marriage may be solemnised between 8am and 6pm on almost any day in the following three months.

2. *Marriage by Common Licence.* This is where the three weeks necessary for the reading of the banns are not available for some reason. One of the couple needs to live in the parish where the marriage will take place, and the residential qualification is only fifteen days immediately prior to the application. One day's clear notice is necessary for the ceremony. The licence is valid for three calendar months. Application for a Common Licence is made to the vicar of the church where the wedding is to be held. Only one person need apply for the licence.

3. *Marriage by Special Licence.* This is fairly unusual, and a Special Licence is issued on the authority of the Archbishop of Canterbury through:

>   The Faculty Office
>   1 The Sanctuary
>   Westminster
>   London SW1

This licence is issued usually because neither of the couple fulfils the residential qualifications or because the wedding is to be held in a place not usually authorised for weddings. This may be because of serious illness (ie in hospital).

4. *By certificate issued by a Superintendent Registrar.* Such a certificate is not binding on a vicar who may still insist on the Common Licence being obtained. If such a certificate is available no other legal documentation is necessary. The bride and groom must have resided not less than seven days in their own districts immediately before the notice is entered by the registrar. The certificate is valid for three months. Cost depends on where each of the couple resides.

Civil ceremony (Register Office)

A totally non-religious wedding may be chosen because one or both of the couple may be divorced and therefore not able to marry in church; the couple may be of different religious beliefs or, as in our church, there is no licenced building for us to use, so couples marry in a civil ceremony as a formality and then hold a Christian service of their own. They can write their own vows and organise the celebration from start to finish.

In order to marry in a register office, notice must be given to the Superintendent Registrar in the district where the couple live and where they intend to marry. An application form also needs to be completed. Names, ages, addresses, marital status, occupation, where the marriage is to take place and how long each person has lived in the area are required, along with a declaration stating there is no lawful impediment.

In the case of either the bride or groom being under the age of legal consent (ie eighteen years of age) the consent in writing of both parents/legal guardians is needed. The bride and groom must have lived in the district where they wish to marry for at least the seven days immediately before giving notice to the Superintendent Registrar. In the case of each of the couple living in different districts, applications must be made in each district. If the bride or groom has been married before, a death certificate or decree absolute must be shown to the Registrar.

If no objection is received within twenty-one days, the certificate will be issued by the Superintendent Registrar. The couple may then marry.

It is possible to marry within the twenty-one days if application is made to the Superintendent Registrar for marriage by Certificate and Licence. Only one of the party needs to give notice and only one needs to have resided in the district for at least fifteen days. If no objections are voiced a certificate will be issued one clear working day later and the marriage can take place in the Register Office within three months.

If you are involved with a church which is not Church of England, consult the leadership for advice about the way forward.

Invitations

Having arranged the wedding venue and formal arrangements it is time to send out the wedding invitations. Traditionally the bride's mother arranges the choosing, printing and sending of the invitations. Invitations should be sent out at least six weeks before the wedding but can be sent earlier if desired.

Many stationers provide a printing service and will have several examples of what is available, showing layout and style. A very popular format is:

Mr and Mrs John Smith
request the pleasure of the company of

. . . .

at the marriage of their daughter
Susan Jane
with
Mr George Alan Jones
at All Saints Church, Jamestown
on Saturday 30th April 199X at 2pm
and at a reception afterwards at the
Belvedere Hotel

98 Castle Avenue   R S V P
This quick brown is being used for testing purposes.
Jamestown Sussex

If the bride's mother is dead the invitation will read:

Mr John Smith
requests the pleasure...

If the bride's father is dead the invitation will read:

Mrs Gillian Smith
requests the pleasure...

The invitations may be sent from parents who are divorced and should read:

Mr John Smith and Mrs Gillian James
request the pleasure...

Invitations to a Register Office wedding follow the same format.

If neither parent will be hosting the wedding the names of the hosts for the occasion should be at the top of the invitation.

It is essential to include RSVP because the hostess needs to know how many guests to expect and cater for. Replies should follow the same format as the invitation. For example:

[Address]

Mr and Mrs Simon Jones
thank Mr and Mrs John Smith for their kind invitation to their daughter's wedding at All Saints Church on Saturday 30th April and to the reception afterwards and are happy to accept.

15th March 199X

No signature is necessary.

Separate invitations may be sent for an evening reception, again following the same format.

Mr and Mrs John Smith
request the pleasure of the company of
. . . .
at the marriage of their daughter
Susan Jane
with
Mr George Alan Jones
at All Saints Church, Jamestown
on Saturday 30th April 199X
at 1.30pm
and at an evening reception at the
Belvedere Hotel
from 7.30pm

98 Castle Avenue   RSVP
Jamestown
Sussex

Prior to sending invitations a comprehensive guest list needs to be compiled. The invitations are sent by the bride's parents and therefore the groom's parents need to supply them with the names and addresses of relatives and friends they would like included.

Present list

At the same time as sending out the invitations a present list needs to be compiled.

Many large stores have a facility to hold your wedding list for you. This means that a list is compiled by you in consultation with the store. It is a detailed list giving specific designs and makes of items, and whenever an item is purchased for you at that store it is crossed off the list. It goes some way to ensuring that you don't get six toast racks or twenty-four assorted egg cups! Some people make someone responsible for the wedding list (eg chief bridesmaid, one of the mothers, a good friend) to whom all communication over presents should be made. Again, this can be a most efficient method.

A detailed list needs to be drawn up. It should give product, manufacturer, style, colour and where it is obtainable. It can also be most helpful to give the price (or approximate price) of each item. It is easiest to list requirements room by room. Here are some of the items you may wish to include on your list:

Kitchen
Refrigerator
Freezer
Washing machine
Tumble dryer
Cooker
Kettle
Coffee maker
Knives—various
Bread board
Bread bin
Toaster
Slow cooker
Microwave
Mixing bowls
Saucepans and frying pan
Tea towels
Oven gloves
Can opener
Cooking utensils
Scales
Pressure cooker
Storage jars
Trays
Wooden spoons
Rubbish bin
Washing-up set
Casserole dishes
Spice rack

Bedroom
Bed
Pillows
Sheets

Living room
Suite (chairs, sofa)
Vases
Lamps
Cushions
Occasional tables
Clock
Rugs
TV

Dining room
Table
Chairs
Place mats
Tablecloth
Dinner service
Tea service
Everyday china
Salt and pepper pots
Cutlery
Glasses—sherry, wine,
          tumblers
Sideboard
Candlesticks
Hot serving plate

Miscellaneous
Vacuum cleaner
Sweeping brush
Dustpan and brush
Garden tools
Garden furniture
Barbecue
Wastepaper bins

Duvet
Duvet covers
Pillow cases
Blankets
Bedspread
Electric blanket
Radio alarm/tea maker

Luggage
Mower
Ornaments

Bathroom
Towels
Mirror
Bathroom cabinet
Linen basket
Bathroom scales
Towel rail

Cheques are always very welcome as you can then buy what you need and want.

This is by no means exhaustive but it gives a good basis from which to work. It is a good idea to include items of varying price to suit all pockets.

Cars

Traditionally the bride's mother is responsible for ordering the wedding cars to take the bride and her father, the bridesmaids and herself to the service. The bridegroom should arrange transport for himself and the best man to the church, and the 'going away' transport for himself and his wife. If the reception is not within walking distance of the church the best man should arrange for the transportation of all guests from the church to the reception. This can usually be done quite informally but the best man should ensure that no one is left behind. Usually the car which transported the bride and her father to the church now takes the newly-wed couple to the reception. The bridesmaids travel in the car in which they arrived. Everyone else travels in their own cars, the bride's parents having arranged for their card to be at the church!

It is not necessary to pay a lot of money and hire cars. Friends will often oblige and use their cars, beautifully cleaned and bedecked with white ribbon. Specialist cars are, however, available to be hired.

Flowers

Flowers are a traditional part of all weddings nowadays. There are flowers to be carried, flowers to be worn and flowers to be displayed. Again the bride's mother is responsible for the wedding bouquets, buttonholes for the men involved and corsages for the two mothers. These can be ordered from a florist or made at home. Care should be taken to co-ordinate colour. There are also church decorations. These need not be on a very grand scale and often there are church members who are willing to use their skills in this way. Attention should be paid to the overall colour scheme.

Table decorations at the reception are also the bride's mother's responsibility and again either a florist or talented relations or friends will do this task. These floral arrangements should be at the reception venue on the morning of the wedding.

Many brides like to have fresh flowers adorning the wedding cake and these should be delivered at the same time as the reception flowers.

Fees

A wedding entails various fees depending on where you marry and in what tradition. These fees do change from time to time and should be checked to ascertain the exact amount payable. Church authorities will be able to let you know this, as will civil authorities. However much payable it is important that the bridegroom has either cash or a cheque book to clear any outstanding debts.

Ushers

The ushers are chosen by the bridegroom from among his male friends. It is also common to include male relatives of the groom and bride. Depending on the size of the church, four are normally sufficient. They should arrive at the church first and hand an Order of Service to each guest. Guests should be shown to their seats, the usher having first ascertained whether they are relatives or friends of the bride or groom. (Seating arrangements are explained later.)

Ushers dress in similar clothing to the bridegroom and best man, ie in morning suits or lounge suits. They are provided with buttonholes.

Music

The music for a wedding is entirely up to the bride and groom in consultation with the church musician(s). It is necessary to choose music to be played before the ceremony; for the bride and her father to walk in to; hymns and songs during the service; music to be played during the signing of the register, and music to leave the church by. There are many 'traditional' pieces which are very popular but some couples choose music which is special to them.

Rings

Traditionally the groom buys a ring for his bride and these days many brides also buy a ring for the groom. It is important for the engagement ring and the wedding ring to be the same carat gold so that one does not wear the other away.

At the service the best man is the custodian of the ring(s) until called upon by the officiating minister. They are then usually placed on a prayer book or Bible. The bride should wear her engagement ring on the third finger of her right hand during the service but she should tell the groom beforehand so he doesn't get confused.

Seating at church

As guests arrive at the church, they should be greeted by an usher and handed an Order of Service if one has been printed. If the guests are unknown to the usher he should enquire whether they are the bride's or groom's guest and he should then escort them to the appropriate seats. Relatives and friends of the bride sit on the left facing the front of the church and relatives and friends of the groom sit on the right. The closer the relationship, the nearer the front the guests should sit.

It is a good idea to reserve seating for young attendants who may find it too long to stand during the whole service. If there is to be an address, chairs or pews may be needed for the bride and groom on the groom's side of the church.

Order of Service

A printed Order of Service is optional but many young people like to keep them as a lasting momento of the occasion. They may be obtained from the same outlets as invitations. The front cover may be a design similar to the invitations. The Order of Service should clearly state what is happening when, and can also contain additional information such as what music is being played and who is taking part in the service. Hymns may be printed in full or hymn books used with just the number given in the Order of Service. If you are having them printed in full, bear in mind that newer songs/choruses are usually copyrighted and permission to use them needs to be sought. This is usually granted free of charge but an acknowledgement is required. It is important to leave enough time for the printing of the Order of Service.

Witnesses

In order to comply with the law a marriage must be witnessed by two people over the age of eighteen. It is customary for the best man and chief bridesmaid to 'do the honours' of signing the register as witnesses but any adults are eligible to do so. If you are choosing other people they must accompany you to the vestry for the signing of the register. Do ensure that there is a working pen for this deed!

Confetti

Many churches object to confetti being thrown within the church grounds. Find out beforehand and spread the word. It is often a good idea to ensure that instructions are given either at the beginning or end of the wedding service. A good alternative (and cheaper too) is rice (not the tinned, creamed variety) or fresh rose petals, both of which are biodegradable! Confetti is thrown as the bride and groom leave for the reception and also when they leave for their honeymoon. It may be a lasting memory, especially as it takes years finally to get rid of every last bit!

Who stands where?

The bride enters the church on her father's right arm. They are followed by page-boys(s) and bridesmaids. The groom stands at the front of the church towards the right, with his best man on his right and slightly behind him. The bride and her father walk down the aisle to the front.

The bride stands next to the groom and passes her bouquet to a bridesmaid. The bride's father stands to her left and slightly behind.

```
                        X   minister
            bride X                X groom
bride's father X                              X best man
bride's friends          X       X
and relations
                                      groom's friends
                                      and relations
. . . . . . . . . . . . . .    bridesmaids      . . . . . . . . . . . . . .
. . . . . . . . . . . . . .      pages          . . . . . . . . . . . . . .
```

When leaving the church, the positions are as follows:

```
            bride's father/groom's mother
                   X           X
Bride's friends                          Groom's friends
and relations      groom's  bride's      and relations
                   father   mother
                   X           X
                 other attendants
                        X
            X                    X
          Best man/chief bridesmaid
              X           X
            Groom       Bride
              X           X
```

Photos/video

Every new bride enjoys looking at the photos of the big occasion. In years to come the album may be quite an historical archive denoting changes in fashion!

Professional photographs are expensive but look good. A photographer will often start at the bride's house, photographing the radiant bride and her father, before going to the church to photograph the groom, best man and other attendants. Some photographers will also photograph the guests arriving. This all, of course, has to be paid for. Many people these days also have a video of their wedding day. There are many professional video companies to be found in *Yellow Pages*. Some churches allow photography and filming during the service, but do check first. After the ceremony, many group photos are taken. A little thought and a carefully drawn up list can result in a very interesting photographic record. Depending on your guest list, of course, how about a group of groom's friends and bride's friends with the newly-weds, or school friends of the couple? Most families like to have traditional groups as well.

One factor to consider is how long the photography will take. It can be very tedious and tiring.

It is not essential to spend a lot on a photographic record. There are usually many amateur photographers snapping away and there may be one who could act as official photographer for the day.

Receiving line

Once everyone has arrived at the reception it is time to be 'received'. This is very informal and gives an opportunity for everyone to say hello to the main personalities. A receiving line is composed thus:

Bride's mother	Bride's father	Groom's mother	Groom's father	Bride	Groom
X	X	X	X	X	X

The best man and chief bridesmaid may also be included but the best man is often busy at this time and the chief bridesmaid is looking after any small attendants.

A receiving line is not absolutely essential and at a very informal wedding may be dispensed with.

After the receiving line guests are offered sherry or a soft drink and move towards the meal.

Seating at the reception

Many receptions are of an informal buffet style. Even at these events there is usually a 'top table' where the main characters involved in the wedding sit.

The bride and groom sit at the head of the table, the bride on her husband's left. The parents and chief attendants make up the rest of the top table:

(A) Chief bridesmaid
(B) Groom's father
(C) Bride's mother
(D) Groom
(E) Bride
(F) Bride's father
(G) Groom's mother
(H) Best man

X	X	X	X	X	X	X	X
A	B	C	D	E	F	G	H

If the parents wish to sit next to each other this is quite permissible. At a formal wedding the other guests are seated according to the wishes of the bride and groom. There should be a clear seating plan displayed and place names at each setting.

At an informal buffet it is important to provide chairs for flagging guests, even though they are not allocated.

Speeches

At the end of the meal the best man takes on the role of toastmaster. He calls upon the father of the bride. If the father is not available, or is reluctant to give a speech, a close friend or relative may step in. The speech is kept fairly short and can be quite humorous, referring to episodes in the bride's life. It is also usual to welcome the new son-in-law into the bride's family. Other jovial comments may be made and amusing incidents related before the toast of health and hapiness of the couple.

The groom replies on behalf of his wife and himself. He thanks everyone for coming, his parents for bringing him up, his in-laws for their daughter and the wedding. He concludes by proposing a toast to the bridesmaids. The groom's speech can be humorous or more serious, but again should not be lengthy.

The best man responds on behalf of the bridesmaids. His speech should be light and definitely humorous. There is rarely any serious content in this speech and it may well recount incidents in the groom's life. A wedding is a happy occasion so there should be no nasty comments. The best man concludes by reading messages of congratulation which have been sent. The major point is always to avoid longwindedness and therefore boredom.

The cake

The wedding cake is often displayed as the centrepiece at the reception. Traditionally this is a rich fruit cake but we have been to one wedding where the cake was an ice-cream gateau and to another where one tier of the cake was sponge because the bride didn't like fruit cake. A wedding cake can be one, two, three or more tiers and it can be any shape. Only small pieces are served.

The cake is often made by one of the mothers and could be iced by them or done professionally. It is worth making a fruit cake three months before in order for it to mature.

The cake is cut after the speeches. The bride and groom place the tip of the knife into the middle of the bottom tier and make a cut. There is usually much posing for the photographs! At this point the cake is removed and cut into pieces which are distributed by the brides-maids.

Cake is often sent to people unable to attend the wedding in small boxes available from the stationers. The bride's mother is responsible for this. It is traditional to save the top tier of the cake as a christening cake for the first child.

Evening reception

Many young couples also hold an evening reception. This enables more people to come and join the celebrations. Food of a snack nature is usally provided, as is drink, but often a bar is in operation.

The bride and groom need to change from their wedding finery into 'going away' outfits. A room should be available for this. The best man should ensure that the groom's clothes are either taken to his new home or returned to the hire shop. The bride's mother should take care of her daughter's wedding clothes.

When the time has come for the couple to leave the reception they should bid farewell and then leave. In many cases the car has been lavishly decorated but hopefully not mechanically interfered with. It is a great relief to drive away together leaving everyone else behind!

The guests may now drift away, having thanked thanked their hosts (the bride's parents) for a most enjoyable day.

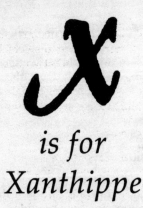

is for
Xanthippe

WELL, WHEN YOU NEED an appropriate word beginning with 'x' you have to settle on something. It wouldn't be a bad idea for you to take a guess at the meaning before reading on to the next paragraph where all will be revealed.

It would be lovely to hear all the imagined meanings, but the word is actually a name. It is the name of the wife of Socrates. We never met the woman since Socrates actually lived from 470-399 BC His wife's dates have eluded us. For some reason his wife's name has found its way into the English language and is defined as, 'a shrewish wife.' This itself being translated suggests she was given to scolding a lot and hence not very nice to live with. There is no mention as to whether Socrates deserved it. One thing's for sure: it is rather shrewish and no doubt the RSPCA will take up this issue on behalf of our animal friends in due course.

So why is it included in this book, interesting though such information is? Quite simply because in these days of sexual equality it is essential to address the whole sexist issue and explore contemporary role models for effective marriages. Have you discovered each other's perspectives or prejudices about the other sex? Work

180

through the following statements individually answering 'yes' or 'no', then discuss your answers. It is important to be honest rather than give what you assume will be the right or acceptable answer.

1. Women are irrational
2. Men are impatient
3. Women are the weaker sex
4. Men are the major breadwinners
5. Women should look after the home
6. Men must exercise ultimate financial responsibility
7. It doesn't matter if the woman doesn't enjoy sex
8. The car is the man's but the woman can use it
9. The kitchen is the woman's domain
10. Sex is initiated by the man
11. Women want to be dominated
12. Men are looking for a substitute mother

It is very easy to pick up stereotypic views about the opposite sex. Growing up, we are surrounded by many exasperated and often negative comments about our fathers by our mothers and vice versa. In an increasing number of situations mums have been left. Homes have entertained a succession of 'uncles', all interested in the carnal delights of the situation, none wanting to accept responsibility for the situation and the people caught up in it.

It is our view that men and women are coequals with gender distinctives and as such none of the above statements can be said to be true. We have found that we complement each other; Katey's strengths compensating for Mike's weaknesses and Mike's strengths for Katey's weaknesses. As one example of this, when Katey met Mike she discovered he was a liability in company. He had no small talk and when he did get involved in conversation it was to argue some keenly felt political point with a passion and commitment which frightened the rest of the company from wanting to risk speaking to him again.

For Katey, who was a most sociable animal, this was somewhat awkward. However, using her skills and experience she took Mike in hand and helped him to own his insecurities and recognise he lacked very much experience in how to act in a social gathering. She also explained that the ferocity and intensity of his conversation made people anxious about chatting with him, so he became something of a social pariah. In spite of the intricate difficulties of communicating this, and regular irrational explosions from Mike, Katey stuck to her task and Mike is now quite well socialised; he is also not uncomfortable in company. A weakness has been converted into a strength. This is one of the benefits of partnership and is a sure sign of a strong marriage.

Interestingly, although the Christian church has often been accused of sexism, when one turns to the Bible one discovers that God, whatever else He might be, is no sexist. In Genesis, the first book in the Bible, it is clear that God made mankind in His own image: 'So God created man in his own image, in the image of God he created him; male and female he created them' (Genesis 1:27).

Therefore at the heart of the Christian faith, which has down the centuries shaped the culture and society of the UK, is the clear recognition that men and women are coequals. Neither is more significant or greater than the other. In fact they are created for mutual interdependence or as a team!

While society at large struggles to respond to the challenge that it is sexist from top to bottom, ie that women occupy very much second place from the world of work to life within the home, our marriages ought to be the place where the coequality of the sexes is practised. Hence prejudices revealed through the statements at the start of this chapter will need to be addressed and dealt with.

For this to operate at any practical level we will need to challenge each other when such prejudices reveal themselves. We should also take initiatives to help change our own mindset where we discover it is suspect.

When we were first married Mike would only allow Katey to help with the decorating by painting skirting boards. These were virtually unnoticeable and so if badly done wouldn't be of any significance. Mike operated on two assumptions: (a) Decorating is men's work not women's, (b) Katey therefore would be less competent than he was.

Such assumptions create attitudes and these attitudes, communicated indirectly, can hurt and rob our partner of their self-worth and dignity. In this case it also meant the decorating took much longer. To change, Mike had to unlearn his assumptions and get rid of his prejudice. Ask yourself whether there are things within your new home together that you wouldn't trust your partner with doing or believe that they would not make as good a job of it as you. A pause for reflection and perhaps discussion might prove constructive!

Marriage is intended as a partnership—both parties co-operating in shaping a relationship, making a home and sustaining friendships. Set views about the general weaknesses of women or men can seriously interfere with the ability of such a partnership to develop realistically. If unresolved, many nagging tensions emerge and one or both members of the marriage are forced to look outside the relationship in order to find approval and value in those areas in which their partner is unable to provide it.

Role models

Most of our prejudices are revealed by our behaviour and values (see 'V is for Values'). Hence when most couples get married they carry into their marriage the prejudices that they have grown up under in their family home and what they have observed in the circles within which they mixed. However, there is no guarantee that such patterns practised by parents are the sum total of correctness or the only model upon which to work out life.

Returning from a trip to Nigeria some years ago, Mike learned from Katey while travelling in the car from Heathrow Airport that she had signed up for a TOPS course in shorthand typing. This raised some interesting questions. We were living in a rented flat at the time and had monthly overheads of rent, bills and housekeeping to meet. Mike was self-employed and generating enough income most months on which to live. Katey had been assisting in the administration side of Mike's work as well as running the flat.

In discussion together we decided to reverse roles. Katey would be paid a small amount while studying and would need to work evenings on homework in order to keep up with what was a short-term, high pressure course of only twelve weeks. That's where the fun really began.

Each morning Mike dutifully drove Katey to the station before returning to housework, shopping and preparing that evening's meal. Late afternoon he would return to collect Katey from the station. Often we would be having guests around to eat during the evening. Whenever Katey got back into the flat she would start ferreting around in the kitchen, anxious about what we would be eating, more for our guests' sake than her own. Mike would have to sternly order her out of the kitchen and, placing a cup of tea in her hand, tell her to have a rest before getting down to the homework.

This went very well, apart from the fact that Mike was not such an economical shopper as Katey was! Over this period Mike's confidence in his cooking skills blossomed and he has continued to be very active in the kitchen. Not just cooking exotic social feasts but the basic everyday meals. This has been helpful as Katey is teaching full time again now so whoever gets in first or is least tired gets together a tasty bite to eat.

It is helpful to explore different role models to those with which we were surrounded as we grew up. At time of writing our household has grown to include a solo mum and her daughter. Deserted by her husband when seven months pregnant she turned to us as friends and we said, 'Come and join the family!' This has meant many more changes, including a move of house to accommodate us all the more easily. Unusual it may be but better by far than a solo mum struggling to bring up a child completely on her own with the minimal income that maintenance affords. As a family we have one budget from which we all live. We believe this model needs to be adopted more widely in order to respond to the type of society that disintegration of marriages and families generates.

Exploration of such models enables others around us, including our own children eventually, to see what it is to live a radical married life in active co-operation and partnership with our husband or wife.

In conclusion we may discover that we find ourselves living under the shadow of our family upbringing—unable to break from certain patterns of behaviour, even though we would like to; locked into certain prejudices we can't shed. If this is the case then we should honestly talk things through together and get some advice and help from a trusted friend. We have found the counsel and prayer of mature Christian friends to help us at this level and would commend talking to a committed Christian leader. Details of someone near you could be provided by writing to us care of the publishers.

*is for
Year*

I T IS OFTEN REMARKED that the first year of marriage is the hardest. This no doubt sounds a little
daunting as you are about to set out on your marriage.
However, there is a measure of truth in the statement.

We believe that marriage has got easier the longer our
relationship has run. On reflection the first year was the
hardest of all, yet this is hardly surprising. Two people
are suddenly forced to work out their lives together
under one roof and with a publicly expressed commitment to each other.

It is certainly only once we are married that a number
of the personal habits and attributes of our partner
become apparent. How could we have been so blind up
to this point, we ask ourselves? All the processes of communication and negotiation are being set in place. The
novelty of being married soon wears off. It now comes
down to grit and determination. Our commitment to
both our partner and our marriage is placed under the
microscope.

In our first year Mike had to learn how to control his
temper (overreaction and unkind retorts to Katey were
the norm over that first year). This demanded a strong
commitment to sustaining the relationship. It also caused

us both to explore precisely what we meant when we said we loved each other. Was this love capable of absorbing the hurtful things we did to each other?

The Bible helped here when we discovered the characteristics of love:

> Love is patient, love is kind. It does not envy, it does not boast, it is not proud. It is not rude, it is not self-seeking, it is not easily angered, it keeps no record of wrongs. Love does not delight in evil but rejoices with the truth. It always protects, always trusts, always hopes, always perseveres. Love never fails (1 Cor 13:4–8).

These words are found in the New Testament of the Bible. They deserve a close reading. Certainly when we considered them we began to understand what love was all about. Indeed, so closely did we keep to them that we can remember the phrase that we learned off by heart from the Authorised Version of the Bible: 'Love bears, believes, hopes and endures all things. Love never fails.'

When Mike had stormed out or Katey had retreated into herself and so was non-communicative, these words reminded us of our commitment to love each other and the goal we were heading for. Knowing these things was not sufficient in and of itself. We had to take practical steps in the light of what we knew. This cost us and every time we each had to take a decision, 'Will I take this step or have I had enough?'

At weddings the words quoted above from the Bible are often chosen as a reading by the bride and groom. In the context of the service, white dresses and all the paraphernalia of the wedding day, they are often listened to with a sentimental 'ooh that's lovely' attitude. We smile to ourselves because for every couple who consider what is being said, and are prepared to adopt it as their definition of love, there is a hazardous and hard journey to make.

187

Wedding anniversaries

Assuming you make it through the first year then it is well worth while celebrating your wedding anniversary. The joke frequently made that husbands don't remember the date and constantly disappoint their wives can easily be circumvented by ensuring one of you write it in his diary. When we get our diaries we always write it in straight away. Mike puts a warning in one week ahead so that he can make suitable purchases if appropriate.

Of all the celebrations in our household (birthdays, Christmas, etc) we make our wedding anniversary the special one. We may not get each other a present but we will do something special to mark the occasion. On our tenth wedding anniversary we found ourselves up a tree house on safari in Zimbabwe. It was more luxurious than it sounds, with electric blankets and hot and cold running water! Many have wondered at the type of tree house this must have been.

Then on our thirteenth anniversary we were shown our very first wild badgers by friends we were visiting. Many memories to enjoy, talk about and reminisce over long into the future.

The difficulty with things like anniversaries is that we can think that we need to spend a fortune. Certainly our cash conscious, prestige hungry society suggests that somehow we should be dining in some exclusive, romantic restaurant supping champagne and indulging ourselves. The inference is that if the men don't initiate at this level then they don't really love their wives. This can generate a sense of guilt, produce a large overdraft or lead us to make unhelpful comparisons with others and the way they 'always' celebrate.

We would recommend that you celebrate in a way that makes economic sense, always remembering that the day is your day. There is no one to impress. It is meant to be for your enjoyment. We would encourage you to follow these guidelines:

Be imaginative. Think of something unique and creative to mark the occasion and to demonstrate your love for your partner. One year Mike literally had no spare cash so he used a promotional photograph of a marquee as an anniversary card. It did have the fact that it was the only such card in the world to recommend it. Katey should have felt special! It's not what you give but the way that you give it that counts.

When deciding how to celebrate together either select one of you to lay on a surprise or co-operate together. The most imaginative treat we have heard of concerned a wife who informed her husband that she was taking him to the races for the day. Not having any money he was suitably impressed. They got dressed appropriately and left to catch the train. Arriving at their destination station the lady concerned marched off away from the ticket barrier and set up stools at the end of the platform. This overlooked the racecourse and with binoculars in hand and a well packed picnic they enjoyed a good day out at the races! And on very much of a shoestring budget.

If you are planning a romantic meal and want to cut corners to remain solvent then allow your imagination to run riot. On one occasion Katey secured a major bargain at the market. Passing a pet stall she spotted some lovely chicken (the dead variety). Enquiring why it was on the pet stall rather than the butcher's the stallholder informed her that as it was bruised it was deemed unfit for human consumption. Pressing him further she discovered that there was nothing else wrong with it and promptly made a purchase. We enjoyed a lovely chicken meal and have been barking ever since!

All the trimmings for that romantic evening can easily be assembled. If necessary, borrow a music machine and cassettes off friends. Make paper flowers or settle for some attractive greenery and unusual coloured plants from the hedgerow. Paint an old milk bottle for service as a candle holder if you haven't any old wine bottles. Katey spied some nice wine bottles in wicker holders hanging from the ceiling of an Italian restaurant and persuaded a waiter to cut her down several. We still use one to this day, the bottle thickly coated in candle wax making it look most appropriate as a table decoration.

A box of wax crayons is a useful investment so that scraps of paper can be decorated by your fair hand and used as wrapping paper or turned into a card with a very personal touch. Unique place mats can also be provided. To be honest, setting up such a meal is so much fun, and has so much of yourselves invested in it, that the whole evening is often more romantic and affirming than the £40 a head job at the local high class restaurant.

Be thoughtful. This is your day. Do be aware that you are celebrating the fact that you have been together. Even if you are returning from a hard day at work make this an occasion. Positively build each other up, and receive with great delight any gift, be it gold-plated cufflinks or bicycle clips. Each of you should find a time to express your appreciation of the other. Think through how you want to express this. It is not a duty to be performed but something you desire to communicate out of the affection you have for your partner.

A further idea is to keep a scrapbook of bits and pieces which reflect the previous year of marriage: stubs from the cinema outing, a postcard of somewhere visited, a slyly taken photo of your spouse. This demonstrates a care and an interest in the year and lays a foundation for building into the year ahead.

Be reflective. Talk through all the things for which you have to be thankful from the previous year. Also note those challenges which changing circumstances have brought, eg deterioration of health or the arrival of children. Take some time to talk around these and stop for a moment of prayer, giving thanks to God and requesting his strength and assistance for the future.

In conclusion, make your anniversary a celebration of marriage. Take time to appreciate one another. Don't lose sight of the event in an orgy of present giving and high entertainment. Rather thank your partner for putting up with you and renew your marriage promises privately to each other. If you are aware of a measure of drift between you both then take agreed steps to change that. In this way anniversaries can provide a wonderful oasis amid the pressures of everyday life and a useful stock take of where you both stand.

As a matter of interest we have reproduced the traditional way anniversaries have been known. The idea is that you purchase a gift of the substance specified.

Anniversary

1st	Cotton	45th	Sapphire
2nd	Paper	50th	Gold
3rd	Leather	55th	Emerald
4th	Silk	60th	Diamond
5th	Wood		
6th	Iron		
7th	Wool		
8th	Bronze		
9th	Pottery		
10th	Tin		
12th	Linen		
15th	Crystal		
20th	China		
25th	Silver		
30th	Pearl		
35th	Coral		
40th	Ruby		

is for
Zero, Blast Off!

APOLOGIES FOR THE CORNY title, but you have made it to the end of the A-Z. Hopefully you are now fully equipped for a life of marriage together. From this point you will be blasting off into your new life together.

Our whole intention with this A-Z has been to provide a practical manual to help and encourage couples like yourselves to set off into marriage on a sure foundation. We realise it is hardly likely you have read this book from cover to cover. It wasn't designed for that. However, we trust that you will keep it by you and make frequent reference to it. It contains a host or practical advice and essential principles to help you in your life together.

Ideally you should pick it up from time to time for a refresher course. Also, when you hit an area of difficulty or some question rears its head, then you will flick through these pages to find some helpful advice.

Our hope and prayer for you both is that you establish a strong marriage and that it provides an enriching experience—not only for you but for those who have the privilege of visiting your home over the years.

God bless you as you set out on the adventure of a lifetime!